Scapegoated

You Were Never The Problem: The Hidden Truth About Narcissistic Family Systems, Emotional Survival, and Finding Yourself on the Other Side

Lynn Nichols

Creative Media Enterprises

This book contains discussions of childhood trauma, emotional and psychological abuse, family dysfunction, and complex PTSD. Some content may be difficult to read or hear, particularly for survivors who are early in their healing journey. Please read or listen at a pace that feels safe for you, take breaks when needed, and consider having professional support in place as you work through this material. If you are in crisis, please reach out to a mental health professional or contact your local crisis helpline.

CONTENTS

PREFACE

If you've picked up this book, you're likely questioning something fundamental about your family relationships—something that others might dismiss as "normal family dysfunction" or encourage you to "just get over." You may be wondering if your memories are accurate, if your emotional reactions are appropriate, or if you're somehow responsible for the pain and conflict that seems to follow you wherever you go.

You're not imagining things. You're not overreacting. And you're certainly not alone.

Family scapegoating is a widespread phenomenon that affects millions of people, yet it remains largely invisible in our culture. Unlike other forms of abuse that leave visible marks or clear evidence, family scapegoating operates through subtle psychological manipulation that can be difficult to identify and even harder to explain to others.

The Challenge of Speaking Out

One of the most difficult aspects of being a family scapegoat is that the very systems designed to help and protect often work against you when you try to speak out. Our culture is deeply invested in myths about family loyalty, unconditional love, and the sanctity of family bonds. When you attempt to share your experiences of systematic emotional abuse, you may encounter responses that silence rather than support you.

Professional systems may not recognize the unique dynamics of family scapegoating. Well-meaning therapists might encourage "family reconciliation" without understanding the systematic nature of your mistreatment. Friends may suggest that you "be the bigger person" or "focus on forgiveness" without grasping that what you experienced wasn't simple conflict but calculated psychological warfare.

Even when you find the courage to speak your truth, you may face further ostracization from family members who recruit others to invalidate your experiences. Flying monkeys—extended family and friends who carry out the family's agenda—may pressure you to minimize your experiences or blame you for "causing family drama" by refusing to accept continued mistreatment.

These responses aren't accidental. They serve to protect systems that benefit from your silence and continued participation in dysfunctional dynamics. Speaking out threatens not just your family's false narrative but broader cultural beliefs about family relationships that many people need to maintain their own psychological comfort.

The Power of Knowledge and Awareness

This book exists because knowledge is power, and awareness is the foundation of all meaningful change. While I cannot promise that understanding your experiences will immediately solve your problems or heal your relationships, I can promise that knowledge will give you something invaluable: clarity.

When you understand the systematic nature of family scapegoating, you stop questioning your own sanity. When you learn about trauma bonding, gaslighting, and triangulation, you recognize tactics that seemed confusing or personal as calculated manipulation strategies. When you see how these patterns operate not just in your family but in broader cultural systems, you understand that your struggles aren't evidence of your inadequacy but of your resistance to accepting unacceptable treatment.

This awareness doesn't necessarily lead to dramatic transformation—healing is complex work that happens over time and often requires professional support. But awareness gives you the tools to make informed decisions about your life, your relationships, and your wellbeing based on reality rather than the distorted narratives you may have internalized.

How This Book Approaches Your Experience

"The Scapegoat Journey" is organized into four parts that build understanding progressively: Recognition, Understanding, Processing, and Healing. Each section provides research-based insights presented in accessible language, drawing from trauma research, family systems theory, and multiple therapeutic approaches.

This book takes a survivor-to-survivor approach rather than a clinical one. While it's grounded in evidence-based research, it acknowledges both the personal impact of family trauma and the broader systemic challenges that make healing difficult. It recognizes that your family dynamics don't exist in isolation but are part of larger patterns of power and control that show up throughout our culture.

The goal isn't to fix you—you were never broken. The goal is to provide you with information that helps you understand what happened to you, why it happened, and how these experiences continue to affect your life. This understanding can help you recognize patterns, protect your wellbeing, and make choices that serve your authentic self rather than others' expectations.

Who This Book Is For

This book is for anyone who has ever felt like the "problem" in their family, who grew up walking on eggshells, or who struggles with the lingering effects of being systematically blamed and criticized. It's for those who have been told they're "too sensitive," "hold grudges," or "can't let go of the past" when they try to address legitimate grievances about their treatment.

It's also for supporters—friends, partners, therapists, and others—who want to understand the unique challenges faced by family scapegoats. Understanding these dynamics is crucial for providing meaningful support rather than inadvertently perpetuating harmful myths about family relationships.

You don't need to be at any particular stage of your healing journey to benefit from this information. Whether you're just beginning to question your family dynamics, actively working on healing, or years into your recovery, understanding the systematic nature of what you experienced can provide valuable insights and validation.

A Note About Self-Care

The material in this book may bring up difficult emotions or memories. This is normal and doesn't mean you're doing anything wrong. Healing isn't linear, and understanding can be both liberating and painful. Please go at your own pace and seek professional support if you find yourself overwhelmed.

This book is educational and supportive, but it doesn't replace professional therapy, medical advice, or crisis intervention services. It's designed to supplement your healing work, not substitute for professional care when needed.

Your Courage in Seeking Understanding

The fact that you're reading this book demonstrates tremendous courage. Questioning your family's treatment of you, especially when others dismiss or minimize your experiences, requires strength that shouldn't be underestimated. Many people go their entire lives accepting unacceptable treatment because examining these patterns is too threatening to their psychological stability.

Your willingness to seek understanding, even when it's difficult and even when others discourage it, is evidence of your resilience and your commitment to living authentically. This courage has brought you this far, and it will carry you through whatever insights and decisions lie ahead.

You deserve to understand your own experience. You deserve to have your reality validated. And you deserve to make informed choices about your life based on truth rather than the distorted narratives others may have created about who you are and what you deserve.

Your journey toward understanding begins here.

1

YOU WERE THEIR CHOSEN VICTIM

UNDERSTANDING FAMILY SCAPEGOATING AND YOUR MOMENT OF RECOGNITION

If you've picked up this book, there's a good chance you've spent most of your life feeling like something was fundamentally wrong with you. Maybe you were told you were "too sensitive," "too difficult," or "the problem child." Maybe you've always felt like the odd one out in your family, the one who just couldn't seem to get it right no matter how hard you tried.

I want to start by telling you something that maybe no one has ever said to you before: **It wasn't your fault. You were their chosen victim.**

My name is Lynn, and I was the family scapegoat too. For decades, I carried the weight of my family's dysfunction on my shoulders, believing that somehow, if I could just be better, do more, or change who I was fundamentally, my family would finally love and accept me. It took me years to understand that the problem was never me—it was the role I was forced to play in a deeply dysfunctional family system.

When I finally had my awakening, when that light switch went on in my brain and I understood what had really happened to me, it was both life-saving and absolutely devastating. Everything suddenly made sense—why I felt so different, why nothing I did was ever good enough, why I always felt like I was walking on eggshells. But with that clarity came the crushing realization that the people who were supposed to love and protect me had systematically chosen me to carry their shame, their dysfunction, and their unprocessed pain.

You were chosen too. Not because you were bad, difficult, or flawed, but because you possessed qualities that threatened their dysfunction. Your empathy, your sense of justice, your emotional awareness, your independence—these beautiful parts of you made you dangerous to their carefully constructed lie that everything was fine.

What Family Scapegoating Really Is

The word "scapegoat" comes from an ancient Hebrew ritual described in the Bible. On the Day of Atonement, two goats were chosen by the high priest. One was sacrificed as an offering, while the other—the scapegoat—was symbolically loaded with all the sins and guilt of the entire community and then sent into the wilderness to die. The community could then feel cleansed and righteous, having transferred all their shame and wrongdoing onto an innocent victim.

In families, this same psychological mechanism plays out with devastating precision. The family scapegoat becomes the repository for all the family's problems, dysfunctions, and uncomfortable emotions. But here's what's crucial to understand: this isn't just a metaphor or a way of speaking. There are real psychological and neurological processes happening here that have been validated by scientific research.

Family scapegoating is a systematic form of emotional abuse where one family member—usually a child—is designated as the cause of all family problems, regardless of logic, evidence, or their actual involvement. It's not occasional unfairness or normal family conflict. It's a deliberate, ongoing pattern of:

- **Blame assignment** that defies logic

- **Emotional dumping** where you become the family's garbage can for uncomfortable feelings

- **Identity attacks** that make you question your fundamental worth

- **Isolation tactics** that separate you from potential allies

- **Psychological manipulation** designed to keep you in the victim role

- **The Moment of Recognition: When the Light Switch Flips**

There comes a moment for many scapegoats when everything suddenly clicks into place. It might happen when you're reading an article about family dysfunction, talking to a therapist, or having a conversation with a friend who points out how abnormal your family stories sound. Suddenly, you see your entire childhood with new eyes.

This moment of recognition is both a blessing and a curse. It's a blessing because finally, finally, you have an explanation for why you felt so crazy, so wrong, so fundamentally flawed for so many years. The confusion lifts. The pieces of the puzzle snap together. You realize you weren't imagining things, you weren't too sensitive, and you weren't the problem.

But it's also devastating because you have to grieve the family you thought you had. You have to accept that the people who were supposed to love and protect you chose to hurt you instead. You have to come to terms with the fact that your pain was not only dismissed but was actually useful to them—it served their psychological needs.

I remember my own moments of recognition. They came in waves over several years, each revelation more shocking than the last. I remember the calm that came with understanding, but also the breathtaking pain of realizing how deliberately I had been hurt. I remember feeling grateful for the truth and absolutely gutted by it at the same time.

If you're having this recognition now, as you read these words, I want you to know that what you're feeling is normal. The relief, the anger, the grief, the confusion—all of it is normal. You're not losing your mind. You're finally seeing clearly.

The Science: You're Not Imagining This

For years, family scapegoats were told they were imagining things, being too sensitive, or making mountains out of molehills. Mental health professionals often dismissed reports of systematic family targeting as "adolescent drama" or "sibling rivalry." But recent research has finally provided scientific validation for what we've always known in our hearts.

In 2023, researchers Martina Vignando and Boris Bizumic published the first empirical study specifically investigating family scapegoating in narcissistic families. Their findings were groundbreaking and confirming:

They studied over 500 adults and confirmed:

- Children of narcissistic parents do indeed get systematically scapegoated

- This scapegoating directly leads to measurable anxiety and depression in adulthood

- The effects are long-lasting and significant, persisting well into adult life

- Both overt (grandiose) and covert (vulnerable) narcissistic traits in parents contribute to scapegoating behaviors

- Maternal grandiose narcissism was particularly linked to scapegoating behaviors

The statistical effects were medium to large, meaning the impact is not only real but substantial and measurable by scientific standards. This isn't subjective interpretation—this is hard data proving that family scapegoating is a real phenomenon with real, lasting consequences.

What this means is that when I tell you that what you experienced was real, I'm not just speaking from my own experience as a fellow scapegoat. I'm telling you that peer-reviewed, published scientific research backs this up. Your experience has been validated by academic study. You're not crazy. You're not too sensitive. You didn't imagine it.

Mental health professionals can no longer dismiss these experiences as subjective complaints or family drama. The science is clear: systematic family scapegoating is a form of psychological abuse that causes measurable harm to children's developing brains and creates lasting mental health challenges in adulthood.

How They Choose Their Victim

One of the most painful questions scapegoats ask is "Why me? What did I do wrong to deserve this?" The answer is both simple and heartbreaking: you did nothing wrong. In fact, you were chosen precisely because of your positive qualities—qualities that threatened the family's dysfunction.

Narcissistic and dysfunctional families don't choose their weakest member to scapegoat. They choose the one who poses the greatest threat to their carefully constructed lies and denial systems. You were chosen because you had qualities that made you dangerous to their dysfunction:

You Had Emotional Intelligence

If you were naturally empathetic and emotionally aware, you were more likely to be targeted. Empathic children feel the family's emotional dysfunction deeply and react to it. They can't pretend everything is fine when it's clearly not. Their emotional reactions become evidence that they're "the problem," when really, they're just reflecting back the family's dysfunction like a mirror.

Your ability to feel deeply, to sense when something was wrong, to react emotionally to emotional situations—these weren't character flaws. These were signs of a healthy, developing emotional system. But in a dysfunctional family, emotional health feels threatening.

You Had a Strong Sense of Justice

Children with an innate sense of fairness become threats to dysfunctional systems. You pointed out inconsistencies and hypocrisies that everyone else was ignoring. You asked uncomfortable questions like "Why is this okay for them but not for me?" You refused to participate in family lies and denial systems. Your honesty threatened the family's carefully constructed facade.

Your sense of right and wrong, your inability to accept obvious unfairness, your insistence on truth—these weren't signs that you were difficult or problematic. These were signs of a healthy moral compass. But moral clarity is dangerous in an immoral system.

You Had Independence and Strong Will

Self-directed children threaten family control systems. You thought for yourself rather than accepting the family narrative without question. You had your own opinions and weren't easily manipulated or controlled. You resisted inappropriate responsibilities and parentification. You showed signs that you might eventually leave the family system entirely—the ultimate threat to their control.

Your independence, your strong will, your refusal to be molded into what they wanted—these weren't character defects. These were signs of a healthy developing sense of self. But autonomy is terrifying to controllers.

You Resembled Someone They Hated

Sometimes the selection process is even more arbitrary and painful. You might have been chosen because you reminded the narcissistic parent of someone they had unresolved anger toward—an ex-partner, their own abusive parent, a sibling they competed with, or even aspects of themselves they couldn't accept.

This is perhaps the cruelest form of selection because it has absolutely nothing to do with who you are or anything you did. You were simply born with the wrong hair color, the wrong facial features, the wrong personality traits, or you were born at the wrong time in their life.

You Were Different in Some Way

Being different in any way could make you a target. Maybe you were more artistic in a "practical" family, more introverted in an extroverted family, more sensitive than they were comfortable with, or had different interests and values. Maybe you had learning differences, health issues, or simply marched to the beat of your own drummer.

Your uniqueness, your individual gifts, your special quali-ties—these weren't problems to be solved. These were treasures to be celebrated. But in families that demand conformity, difference feels dangerous.

The Devastating Moment of Recognition

When you first realize you were the family scapegoat, the emotional impact can be overwhelming. This recognition often comes with a complex mix of emotions that can feel contradictory and confusing:

Relief and Validation

There's often immediate relief when you finally have a name for your experience. All those years of feeling crazy, of doubting your own perceptions, of wondering what was wrong with you—suddenly you have an explanation. You weren't imagining things. You weren't too sensitive. There really was something wrong, but it wasn't you.

This validation can feel like finally being able to breathe after holding your breath for decades. The confusion lifts. The pieces of your life story suddenly make sense. You realize you've been gaslighted for years, and while that's painful, it's also liberating to trust your own perceptions again.

Overwhelming Grief

Along with relief comes devastating grief. You have to mourn the family you thought you had. You have to accept that the people who were supposed to love and protect you chose to hurt you instead. You have to grieve the childhood you deserved but never received, the protection you needed but never got, the love you craved but was always conditional.

This grief is profound and legitimate. You're not just mourning what happened to you—you're mourning what didn't happen. The birthday parties where you felt celebrated, the achievements that were acknowledged, the times you needed comfort and received it, the sense of belonging and safety that should have been your birthright.

Righteous Anger

As the reality sinks in, anger often follows—and it should. You have every right to be furious about what was done to you. They stole your childhood innocence, your sense of safety, your trust in relationships, your confidence in your own perceptions. They robbed you of the secure foundation every child deserves and then blamed you for the instability they created.

This anger is not only justified—it's necessary for healing. It's your internal system finally recognizing that boundaries were violated, that you were treated unfairly, that what happened was wrong. Don't let anyone tell you that you need to "get over it" or "forgive and forget." Your anger is valid and important.

Overwhelming Confusion

Even with understanding comes confusion. How could people who claimed to love you treat you this way? How could other family members witness your pain and do nothing? How could this systematic abuse happen in plain sight while everyone pretended it was normal?

The cognitive dissonance can be intense. Your heart wants to believe they loved you, even while your mind now understands they hurt you deliberately. You may find yourself going back and forth between clarity and doubt, between understanding and confusion.

Terrifying Isolation

Recognition often comes with the stark realization of how alone you really were. Not only were you the target, but there was no one to protect you, no one to validate your experience, no one to intervene on your behalf. The people who should have been your advocates became your persecutors or silent accomplices.

This isolation can feel overwhelming, especially when you realize it may continue. Setting boundaries based on your new understanding often leads to family ostracization, leaving you feeling more alone than ever.

You Are Not Alone

As isolated as you may feel right now, I want you to know that you are part of a community you never asked to join, but one that understands your experience completely. There are thousands of us who have walked this path of recognition and healing.

The study I mentioned earlier included over 500 people, and that's just one study. Online communities for scapegoat recovery have tens of thousands of members. Support groups exist in cities around the world. You are not the only one who experienced this. You are not uniquely broken or uniquely targeted.

What happened to you happens in families across all socioeconomic levels, all cultures, all religious backgrounds. Narcissistic and dysfunctional family systems operate remarkably similarly regardless of other demographic factors. The tactics are the same, the roles are the same, the damage is the same.

This doesn't minimize your individual pain or experience, but it does mean you're not alone in understanding it. There are people who will believe you without question, who will recognize the patterns you describe, who will validate your experience without requiring proof or explanation.

What This Recognition Means Going Forward

Understanding that you were the family scapegoat is both an ending and a beginning. It's the end of accepting blame for things that weren't your fault, the end of believing their story about who you are, the end of hoping they'll change and finally see your worth.

But it's also the beginning of seeing yourself clearly, the beginning of healing from wounds you now understand, the beginning of building relationships based on truth rather than performance, the beginning of reclaiming your authentic self.

This recognition is the first step on a journey that will take you through grief, anger, confusion, healing, and ultimately, empowerment. It's not an easy journey, but it's a necessary one. And you don't have to walk it alone.

In the next chapter, we'll help you identify the specific signs and patterns that confirm your experience. You'll gain even more clarity about what happened to you and why. But for now, just sit with this recognition. You were chosen to be their victim, but you survived. You found your way to this truth. And that means you have everything inside you that you need to heal.

You were never the problem. You were their chosen victim. And now that you know the truth, your real life can finally begin.

2

THE SIGNS THEY MARKED YOU

RECOGNIZING THE PATTERNS OF SYSTEMATIC TARGETING

Now that you understand what family scapegoating is and why you were chosen, you need tools to recognize the specific patterns that confirm your experience. The signs of systematic family targeting are often subtle and woven into the fabric of daily family life, making them seem normal when they're anything but.

Many scapegoats struggle with doubt, even after their initial recognition. You might find yourself thinking, "Maybe it wasn't that bad," or "Maybe I really was difficult." This is normal—you've been conditioned to doubt your own perceptions for years. The gaslighting was so thorough that even when you see the truth clearly, part of you may still question it.

That's why having concrete signs to look for is so important. These aren't subjective interpretations or emotional reactions. These are specific, observable patterns of behavior that distinguish systematic scapegoating from normal family conflict or occasional unfairness.

As you read through these signs, pay attention to your body's response. Your nervous system often recognizes truth before your mind does. You might feel your stomach tighten, your chest constrict, or tears spring to your eyes. These physical reactions are your body saying, "Yes, this happened to me."

The Signs of Systematic Scapegoating

Consistent and Disproportionate Blame

You found yourself consistently blamed for family issues or problems, regardless of your actual involvement or the logic of the situation. This wasn't occasional unfairness—it was a pattern so consistent you could predict it.

If something went missing in the house, you were accused first, even if you weren't home when it disappeared. When there was family conflict, somehow it became your fault regardless of who started it or what the actual issue was. Your siblings could engage in the exact same behavior, but you were the one who got in trouble.

The blame was always disproportionate to your actual involvement. If you left a dish in the sink, it became evidence that you were "selfish and inconsiderate." If your sibling left ten dishes, it was "no big deal" or "they were busy." The punishment never fit the supposed crime and was always excessive when applied to you.

You were blamed for other people's emotions and reactions: "You made Mom cry," "Look what you've done to your father," or "You're stressing everyone out." Family problems that existed before you were born somehow became your responsibility. Even when you were physically absent from situations, negative outcomes were still attributed to your influence.

This happened because the family system needed someone to blame to avoid examining their real problems. You were designated as the cause of all troubles, regardless of logic, evidence, or common sense.

Unreasonable and Constant Criticism

You were the target of relentless criticism, often for trivial, contradictory, or even fabricated reasons. No matter how hard you tried, nothing you did was ever quite good enough. The goalposts constantly moved.

Your accomplishments were systematically minimized: "Anyone could have done that," "You just got lucky," or "It's not that impressive." Your mistakes, however, were magnified and brought up repeatedly, sometimes years later. You became the family's permanent example of what not to do.

The criticism was often contradictory. You were told you were too quiet, then criticized for being too loud. You were called antisocial for spending time alone, then criticized for being too social when you went out with friends. No matter what you did, there was always something wrong with it.

The criticism felt personal and attacked your character rather than addressing specific behaviors. Instead of "Please clean up your room," you heard "You're such a slob." Instead of "Please speak more respectfully," you heard "You're so rude and ungrateful."

Meanwhile, other family members' mistakes were overlooked, excused, or explained away. When your sibling failed a test, they were having a hard time and needed support. When you failed a test, you were lazy and not trying hard enough.

This constant criticism served to keep you off-balance and prevent you from developing confidence or challenging the family system. It maintained your position as the "flawed" one who always needed correction.

Double Standards and Unfair Rules

Rules and expectations were applied more harshly and inconsistently to you than to other family members. What others could get away with, you absolutely could not.

Your siblings could break curfew with minor consequences or explanations, but you faced severe punishment for being five minutes late. You were expected to be more mature, responsible, and understanding than your age warranted, while siblings the same age or older were given more leeway for "childish" behavior.

Your privacy was routinely invaded—your room searched, your diary read, your phone monitored—while others' privacy was respected. You had stricter rules about friends, activities, and freedoms. Your needs were consistently considered less important than everyone else's convenience.

You were expected to apologize even when you were the one who was wronged. If a sibling hurt you and you reacted, you were the one who had to say sorry for "causing drama" or "being too sensitive." You had to "earn" things that others received freely—love, privileges, support, or basic necessities.

These different standards weren't subtle. They were obvious enough that even you could see the unfairness, but when you pointed it out, you were told you were "imagining things" or being "dramatic."

Emotional and Verbal Abuse Disguised as Care

You experienced frequent emotional and verbal abuse that was cleverly disguised as honesty, humor, or helpfulness, making it difficult to identify and impossible to confront.

Insults were delivered as jokes: "I'm just kidding, you're so sensitive!" The "joke" defense allowed them to hurt you while making you the problem if you reacted. "Constructive criticism" was actually character assassination designed to tear down your self-esteem rather than help you improve.

Public humiliation was disguised as sharing "funny" family stories. Your most embarrassing moments became entertainment for others, and if you objected, you were "taking things too seriously" or "can't take a joke."

You experienced extensive gaslighting: "That never happened," "You're remembering it wrong," or "You're being too sensitive." Your feelings were consistently dismissed and invalidated. You were told your perceptions were incorrect: "That's not what I meant" when it clearly was exactly what they meant.

This abuse was particularly damaging because it came with built-in denial. They could hurt you and then claim they were trying to help, being honest, or just having fun. It made you question your own reactions and wonder if you really were too sensitive.

Systematic Isolation and Alienation

You felt profoundly isolated within your own family unit, with limited emotional support or genuine connection from anyone.

You were routinely excluded from family activities, conversations, or inside jokes. Family members would discuss you when you weren't around but never talked directly with you about issues or concerns. Important family decisions that affected you were made without your input or consultation.

During family events, you often felt like you were watching from the outside rather than participating. You might have been physically present but emotionally excluded. Family photos often reflected this—you were positioned separately or your expressions showed your disconnection.

Other family members had obviously closer relationships with each other than they did with you. They shared bonds, experiences, and connections that you were never invited into. You felt like a stranger living with people who happened to share your last name.

This isolation wasn't accidental. It prevented you from forming alliances that might challenge the family system and kept you dependent on their definitions of reality. With no allies within the family, you had no one to confirm your perceptions or validate your experiences.

Projection of All Family Problems

The family's dysfunction was systematically blamed on you, making you responsible for everyone else's problems and emotional states.

You heard statements like "You're the reason Mom and Dad fight," "You stress everyone out," or "The family would be happy if you just..." Your very presence was treated as the source of family tension and unhappiness.

Others' bad moods, problems, or failures somehow became your fault. If your parent was stressed about work, they took it out on you. If your sibling was having friend problems, they blamed you for creating a stressful home environment. You became the family's emotional dumping ground.

You were expected to change your personality, your interests, or your natural reactions so that others could feel better. Your authentic self was treated as an inconvenience or a problem to be solved.

This projection allowed everyone else to avoid taking responsibility for their own emotions, behaviors, or contributions to family problems. As long as you were the designated problem, they never had to examine their own dysfunction.

Parentification and Inappropriate Responsibilities

You were assigned adult responsibilities while being denied adult respect, power, or decision-making authority.

You were expected to manage other people's emotions: "Don't upset your mother," "Your father has had a hard day," or "Your sister is going through a difficult time." Keeping everyone else happy became your job, but no one was responsible for your emotional well-being.

You became the family mediator, expected to solve conflicts between other family members or smooth over tensions. You were held responsible for family harmony while having no actual power to create it.

You might have been put in charge of siblings who were close to your age or even older, but when those siblings misbehaved or got into trouble, you were blamed for not controlling them properly. You had responsibility without authority.

You were expected to be "the strong one" during family crises, supporting everyone else while your own need for support was ignored. You became your parent's confidant about adult problems that were inappropriate for a child to handle.

This inappropriate responsibility served the family's needs while keeping you in a subordinate position. You had all the stress of adult responsibilities but none of the respect or power that should come with them.

Minimization and Dismissal of Your Achievements

Your accomplishments, needs, and emotions were routinely overlooked, minimized, or met with indifference.

Your achievements were consistently downplayed: "It's not that big a deal," "You were just lucky," or "Anyone could have done that." When you succeeded at something, credit was given to your teachers, coaches, or circumstances rather than your effort or ability.

Others often received credit for your accomplishments. If you helped with a family project, someone else was praised for the result. If you contributed to a solution, someone else got the recognition.

Your struggles and difficulties were dismissed: "Other people have it worse," "You don't know how good you have it," or "Stop feeling sorry yourself." Your emotional needs were treated as less important than everyone else's convenience.

Celebrations for your achievements were noticeably smaller, less enthusiastic, or shorter-lived than celebrations for others. Your milestones were forgotten or overshadowed by other family members' less significant accomplishments.

This systematic minimization served to maintain the narrative that you weren't particularly special or valuable, preventing you from developing healthy self-esteem or confidence in your abilities.

Emotional Manipulation and Psychological Control

Sophisticated manipulative tactics were used specifically to control your behavior and keep you in line with family expectations.

You experienced regular guilt-tripping: "After everything I've done for you," "You're breaking my heart," or "How can you be so selfish?" Your natural empathy was weaponized against you to make you comply with unreasonable demands.

Emotional blackmail was common: "You're going to give me a heart attack," "You'll be sorry when I'm gone," or "You're destroying this family." Your actions were framed as having catastrophic consequences for others' well-being.

The silent treatment was used as punishment when you asserted yourself, disagreed, or failed to meet expectations. You were frozen out until you apologized or changed your behavior, even when you had done nothing wrong.

Love-bombing followed by withdrawal kept you confused and constantly seeking approval. One day you were the favorite; the next day you were invisible or in trouble. This intermittent reinforcement created a psychological dependency on their approval.

Triangulation was used to control you—other family members were used to send messages, gather information, or manipulate your behavior. You never knew who you could trust or who was reporting back to the primary abuser.

Truth-Telling is Severely Punished

When you tried to point out family dysfunction, speak honestly about problems, or defend yourself, you faced severe consequences.

Stating obvious facts was labeled as "stirring up trouble" or "causing drama." You were told not to "air the family's dirty laundry" when you sought help from teachers, friends, or other adults about what was happening at home.

Your honesty was reframed as disrespect, ingratitude, or talking back. Defending yourself was treated as a worse offense than whatever you were originally accused of doing.

You were told you were "remembering wrong" when you brought up past incidents of abuse or unfairness. Your perceptions were consistently invalidated, making you doubt your own memory and judgment.

Family secrets and image maintenance were treated as more important than your well-being. You were expected to protect the family's reputation even when it meant accepting ongoing abuse.

This punishment of truth-telling served to maintain the family's denial system and prevent outside intervention. Your voice was the biggest threat to their carefully constructed facade.

Medical and Mental Health Needs Ignored

Your physical and emotional health needs were consistently dismissed, delayed, or blamed on your character rather than treated with appropriate care.

When you were sick or injured, you were accused of faking it, exaggerating, or seeking attention. Medical appointments were treated as inconveniences to the family schedule rather than necessary care.

Mental health struggles were blamed on your "bad attitude," "difficult personality," or "attention-seeking behavior" rather than recognized as symptoms that needed professional support.

Your symptoms were minimized: "It's all in your head," "You're being dramatic," or "Other kids don't complain this much." Self-harm or suicidal thoughts were treated as manipulation rather than signs of serious distress.

Meanwhile, other family members' health needs were taken seriously and addressed promptly. The message was clear: your suffering didn't matter as much as theirs.

Financial Inequality and Conditional Resources

Money, resources, and opportunities were distributed unfairly within the family, with you consistently receiving less or having to meet additional conditions to receive basic support.

Your siblings received more generous allowances, better clothes, more expensive gifts, or more financial support for activities and opportunities. Your needs were labeled as "wants" while others' wants were treated as necessities.

You had to "earn" things that others received freely. Financial support came with strings attached and could be withdrawn at any time as punishment for not meeting behavioral expectations.

Your path to financial independence was often sabotaged. You might have been discouraged from working, had earnings taken away, or been made to feel guilty for achieving financial success.

This financial control maintained your dependency and reinforced your lower status within the family hierarchy.

Identity Attacks and Character Assassination

Rather than addressing specific behaviors, criticism focused on attacking your fundamental character and identity.

You heard statements like "You're just selfish," "You're lazy," or "You're ungrateful"—broad character attacks rather than specific behavioral feedback. These labels became part of how the family referred to you and how you learned to see yourself.

Your motivations were consistently questioned or misinterpreted. If you helped someone, you were accused of showing off. If you didn't help, you were selfish. There was no way to win.

Positive changes in your behavior were attributed to outside influences rather than personal growth: "Your teacher must be making you do that" or "You're just trying to impress someone."

This attack on your identity was more damaging than criticism of specific actions because it made you question your fundamental worth as a person.

Boundary Violations and Privacy Invasion

Your boundaries were consistently crossed while you were expected to respect everyone else's without question.

Your personal space, belongings, and privacy were regularly invaded. Your room was searched, your diary read, your phone monitored, your mail opened. Meanwhile, others' privacy was carefully respected.

You were forced to share personal information when you wanted privacy and excluded from information that affected you. Family decisions that impacted your life were made without your input.

Physical boundaries were violated through forced affection, inappropriate touching, or being made to hug or kiss people when you were uncomfortable. Your "no" was not respected or taken seriously.

These violations prevented you from developing a healthy sense of self and personal autonomy.

Loyalty Tests and Forced Allegiance

You were repeatedly tested for loyalty to the family system and forced to choose between your well-being and family acceptance.

You were expected to defend family members who hurt you and to prioritize family loyalty over your own needs or outside relationships. Seeking therapy or confiding in others about family problems was treated as betrayal.

You were told that if you really loved the family, you would accept the dysfunction without complaint. "Family first" was used to justify ongoing mistreatment.

Extended family members who might have supported you were kept away or turned against you through manipulation and lies.

Crisis Scapegoating

During family emergencies, illnesses, or major stressful events, you somehow became the problem rather than receiving the support you needed.

Family crises were blamed on your behavior or presence. You were expected to handle your own difficulties while supporting everyone else through theirs.

Your normal emotional reactions to trauma or stress were labeled as inappropriate, selfish, or attention-seeking. You were told you were "making things worse" when you expressed natural human emotions during difficult times.

Academic and Professional Sabotage

Your educational achievements and career aspirations were undermined, minimized, or treated as threatening to the family.

Good grades were attributed to luck or easy teachers rather than your intelligence and effort. You were discouraged from pursuing higher education or ambitious career goals.

Family obligations were scheduled to conflict with important academic or professional commitments. Your success was treated as abandonment of the family or "getting too big for your britches."

Social Isolation and Relationship Interference

Your relationships outside the family were discouraged, criticized, or actively sabotaged.

Friends were made to feel unwelcome in your home or were criticized unfairly. You were told your friends were "bad influences" when they treated you well or supported you.

Romantic relationships were undermined through criticism, interference, or creating family conflicts that demanded your attention during important relationship moments.

You were made to feel guilty for spending time with people who treated you well, as if loyalty to anyone outside the family was a betrayal.

Emotional Parentification

You were expected to manage the emotional needs and well-being of family members while your own emotional needs were ignored or dismissed.

You became your parent's confidant about adult problems, marriage issues, or financial stress. You were expected to provide emotional support that was inappropriate for your age and development.

You were made responsible for managing conflicts between other family members and blamed when you couldn't successfully resolve adult problems.

Your own emotional needs were treated as less important than your role as the family's emotional caretaker.

Ostracization After Boundary Setting

When you finally tried to protect yourself by setting boundaries, reducing contact, or speaking up about the abuse, you faced complete ostracization from the extended family system.

Family members who had claimed to love you suddenly treated you with hatred and contempt. Extended family took sides against you without hearing your perspective or witnessing the abuse firsthand.

You were painted as the villain for trying to protect your mental health and well-being. The narrative became that you were "breaking up the family" rather than responding to years of systematic mistreatment.

This final punishment confirmed that their "love" had always been conditional on your acceptance of abuse.

In the next chapter, we'll explore why you specifically were chosen for this role and how the selection process really works. Understanding this will help you see that being targeted was actually a testament to your positive qualities, not evidence of your flaws.

For now, trust what you recognize. Trust your body's reactions as you read these signs. Trust your memories, even if they've been questioned and invalidated for years. Your experience was real, it was systematic, and it was wrong. And now that you can see it clearly, you can begin to heal from it.

3

Why You? The Selection Process

How They Chose You and What It Really Means

One of the most agonizing questions that haunts family scapegoats is "Why me?" You've probably spent countless hours trying to figure out what you did wrong, what was so terrible about you that your own family would single you out for such treatment. You may have convinced yourself that if you could just identify your fatal flaw, you could fix it and finally earn the love you desperately wanted.

I'm here to tell you something that might be hard to believe at first: you weren't chosen because you were bad, difficult, or fundamentally flawed. You were chosen because you were good. You were chosen because you possessed qualities that threatened the family's dysfunction. You were chosen because you were dangerous to their carefully constructed lies.

This truth can be almost harder to accept than believing you deserved the abuse. If you were chosen for your positive qualities, it means your family deliberately targeted someone who didn't deserve it. It means they saw your light and chose to try to extinguish it. It means the abuse was even more calculated and cruel than you realized.

But understanding the real selection process is crucial for your healing. It shifts the narrative from "What's wrong with me?" to "What was wrong with them?" It helps you reclaim the beautiful qualities that made you a target and see them as the gifts they truly are.

The Threat You Represented

Narcissistic and dysfunctional families operate on carefully maintained lies. They need everyone to believe that the family is basically fine, that any problems are minor or caused by external factors, and that the narcissistic parent is a good person who's doing their best. These lies require everyone's participation to maintain.

You were dangerous because you threatened these foundational lies. Your very existence, your natural reactions, your authentic self—all of it challenged the family's false narrative. You couldn't help but reflect back their dysfunction, and that made you a problem that needed to be controlled or eliminated.

You Had Emotional Intelligence and Empathy

If you were naturally empathetic and emotionally aware, you posed a significant threat to the family's emotional dysfunction. Empathic children feel deeply and react authentically to what's happening around them. In a healthy family, this is celebrated and nurtured. In a dysfunctional family, it's terrifying.

Your emotional reactions served as a mirror, reflecting back the family's pain, anger, sadness, and dysfunction. When there was tension between your parents, you felt it and reacted to it. When someone was being treated unfairly, you were disturbed by it.

When love was conditional or manipulative, you sensed it and pulled away.

Your empathy made you incredibly inconvenient. You couldn't pretend everything was fine when it wasn't. You couldn't laugh along with cruel jokes. You couldn't ignore obvious suffering or injustice. Your emotional honesty threatened their emotional dishonesty.

They needed you to stop feeling so much, stop reacting so authentically, stop reflecting back their dysfunction. Since they couldn't make you less empathetic, they decided to make your empathy the problem. They labeled you as "too sensitive," "dramatic," or "emotional" instead of examining why you were reacting to genuine dysfunction.

Your empathy wasn't a character flaw—it was a superpower that terrified them.

You Had a Strong Moral Compass

Children with an innate sense of justice and fairness become immediate threats to unjust family systems. You pointed out inconsistencies, double standards, and obvious unfairness because your internal moral compass couldn't ignore them.

You asked uncomfortable questions: "Why is it okay when they do it but not when I do it?" "Why do I have to apologize when they hurt me?" "Why are we pretending this is normal?" These questions threatened the family's ability to maintain their dysfunctional patterns without examination.

You refused to participate in family lies, denial, or cover-ups. When they tried to rewrite history, you remembered what really happened. When they tried to minimize abuse, you insisted it was serious. When they tried to blame victims, you defended them.

Your moral clarity was dangerous because it exposed their moral bankruptcy. They needed everyone to go along with the lies, the manipulation, the unfairness. Your refusal to participate threatened to bring the whole house of cards tumbling down.

They couldn't corrupt your moral compass, so they decided to make your morality the problem. They labeled you as "self-righteous," "judgmental," or "difficult" instead of examining their own behavior.

Your sense of justice wasn't a character flaw—it was integrity that threatened their corruption.

You Had Independence and Self-Direction

Self-directed children with their own thoughts, opinions, and goals represent an existential threat to controlling family systems. You thought for yourself rather than simply accepting the family narrative. You had your own interests, your own friends, your own dreams.

You resisted attempts to mold you into what they wanted you to be. You pushed back against inappropriate responsibilities, unreasonable expectations, and attempts to control your thoughts and feelings. You showed signs that you might eventually leave the family system entirely—the ultimate threat to their control.

Your independence meant you couldn't be easily manipulated or controlled through the usual tactics. You questioned their authority when it was unreasonable. You maintained relationships outside the family that might provide alternative perspectives. You had your own sources of validation and self-worth.

Your autonomy was terrifying to people who needed to control everything and everyone around them. They couldn't make you dependent on them for your sense of reality, so they decided to make your independence the problem. They labeled you as "rebellious," "disrespectful," or "ungrateful."

Your independence wasn't a character flaw—it was strength that threatened their need for control.

You Were Intellectually Curious and Perceptive

Smart, observant children who ask questions and think critically are dangerous to families built on lies and denial. You noticed inconsistencies in their stories. You remembered things they wished you would forget. You connected dots they didn't want connected.

You might have been the child who asked why Daddy was "sick" every weekend but fine during the week. You might have noticed that Mommy's bruises didn't come from "falling down stairs." You might have observed that the family's public image was very different from their private reality.

Your intellectual curiosity led you to seek explanations for things that didn't make sense. Your perceptiveness allowed you to see through their facades and manipulations. Your ability to think critically meant you couldn't be easily fooled or gaslit.

They needed you to stop noticing, stop asking questions, stop remembering, stop thinking. Since they couldn't make you less intelligent, they decided to make your intelligence the problem. They labeled you as "smart-mouthed," "know-it-all," or "thinks they're better than everyone."

Your intelligence wasn't a character flaw—it was perception that threatened their deception.

You Resembled Their Shadow

Sometimes the selection process is even more arbitrary and cruel. You might have been chosen simply because you reminded the narcissistic parent of someone they hated, feared, or felt inferior to.

Perhaps you looked like an ex-partner they had unresolved anger toward. Maybe you had the same hair color, eye color, or facial features as someone who hurt or rejected them. You might have inherited personality traits from a family member they despised.

Sometimes you represented aspects of themselves that they couldn't accept. If they were ashamed of their own sensitivity, they attacked yours. If they felt guilty about their own selfishness, they projected it onto you. If they feared their own inadequacy, they needed to make you feel inadequate.

You might have been born at the wrong time—during a period of stress, loss, or unwanted change in their life. You became associated with their pain and blamed for circumstances completely beyond your control.

This type of selection is perhaps the cruelest because it has absolutely nothing to do with who you are or anything you did. You were condemned for resembling someone else, for reminding them of their own flaws, or for existing during their difficult period.

You Were Different in Some Way

Being different from the family norm in any way could mark you for targeting. Maybe you were more artistic in a "practical" family, more introverted in an extroverted family, more academically inclined in an anti-intellectual family, or more spiritually minded in a materialistic family.

Perhaps you had learning differences, physical challenges, or health issues that made you stand out. Maybe you were adopted and looked different from the biological family members. You might have been more sensitive, more emotional, or more idealistic than they were comfortable with.

Your differences reminded them that people could be other than what they were. Your uniqueness challenged their narrow definitions of acceptable behavior, interests, or ways of being. Your individuality threatened their need for conformity and control.

Instead of celebrating your unique gifts and supporting your individual development, they decided to make your differences the problem. They tried to force you to conform, criticized your interests, or made you feel ashamed of the qualities that made you special.

Your uniqueness wasn't a character flaw—it was authenticity that threatened their need for conformity.

The Selection Isn't Always Conscious

It's important to understand that the narcissistic or dysfunctional parent doesn't usually sit down and consciously decide to scapegoat a particular child. The selection process is often unconscious, driven by their own psychological needs, unhealed trauma, and defense mechanisms.

They may genuinely believe that you are more difficult, more problematic, or more in need of correction than your siblings. They've convinced themselves of their own narrative through years of projection, rationalization, and self-deception.

This unconscious aspect of the selection makes it even more crazy-making for you. There's no logical explanation you can point to, no moment where they made a deliberate decision to target you. It just gradually became the family's reality that you were the problem child.

But unconscious doesn't mean accidental or unavoidable. The psychological forces at work are powerful and systematic, creating predictable patterns of abuse that are remarkably similar across different families. The unconscious nature of the selection doesn't make it less real or less damaging.

How the Role Gets Reinforced

Once you've been selected as the scapegoat, several psychological and social forces work to reinforce and maintain this role:

Confirmation Bias

The family develops a lens through which everything you do gets interpreted negatively. If you help with chores, you're "showing off" or "trying to make others look bad." If you don't help, you're "lazy" and "selfish." There's no way to win because they're looking for evidence to confirm their existing belief that you're the problem.

Your neutral behaviors get interpreted as negative. Your positive behaviors get dismissed or reframed as manipulation. Your negative behaviors get magnified and used as proof that their treatment of you is justified.

Self-Fulfilling Prophecy

The constant criticism, blame, and negative treatment eventually affects your behavior. You may become withdrawn, defensive, angry, or rebellious—natural responses to ongoing abuse. These reactions then get used as evidence that you really are difficult or problematic.

They create the very behaviors they claim to be responding to. Your trauma responses to their abuse become proof that their abuse was necessary. It's a perfect circular system that justifies itself.

Family Investment

Once the family system organizes around your role as the scapegoat, everyone becomes invested in maintaining it. Your siblings prefer that you remain the target rather than risk becoming targets themselves. The enabling parent avoids conflict by allowing it to continue. The narcissistic parent gets their psychological needs met by having a designated victim.

Changing the dynamic would require everyone to examine their own behavior and take responsibility for their participation in the abuse. It's easier to maintain the status quo and keep you in the designated role.

Trauma Bonding

Paradoxically, the abuse creates a psychological bond that makes it difficult for you to leave or reject the family system entirely. The intermittent periods of kindness or normalcy create hope that things might change. The fear of losing what little connection you have can keep you trapped in the abusive dynamic.

The trauma bonding makes you vulnerable to believing their narrative about you and accepting treatment that you would never tolerate from strangers.

The Role Can Shift or Be Shared

In some families, the scapegoat role isn't fixed permanently on one person. It might shift between children depending on circumstances, family stress levels, or the narcissistic parent's current needs.

You might have been the primary scapegoat most of the time but temporarily "promoted" when the family needed to present a good image or when a sibling did something that couldn't be ignored. Conversely, you might have been the golden child who fell from grace and became the scapegoat.

Some families have multiple scapegoats or rotate the role seasonally. Some have a primary scapegoat and a backup scapegoat who gets targeted when the primary one isn't available.

The fluidity of the role in some families proves that it's not really about your inherent characteristics but about the family's psychological needs at any given moment.

What Your Selection Really Means

Understanding that you were chosen for your positive qualities rather than your negative ones is revolutionary for your healing journey. It means:

You weren't born broken. The qualities that made you a target—empathy, justice orientation, independence, intelligence, authenticity—are actually strengths that the world needs more of.

You weren't too much. You were exactly the right amount of everything you were. They were too little—too little empathy, too little integrity, too little emotional capacity to handle your authentic self.

You weren't the problem. You were the solution that they rejected. You represented healing, growth, truth, and change—everything they were desperately trying to avoid.

You weren't unlovable. You were so lovable that they felt threatened by it. Your capacity for genuine connection and authentic relationship made their shallow, manipulative relationships look inadequate by comparison.

You weren't supposed to be different. You were supposed to be exactly who you are. Your authentic self was never the problem—their inability to accept and celebrate authenticity was the problem.

The family scapegoat is often the healthiest member of the family masquerading as the sickest. You were the one who couldn't pretend everything was fine, couldn't participate in the denial, couldn't accept the unacceptable. In a sick system, health looks like sickness.

Reclaiming Your Targeted Qualities

Now that you understand why you were really chosen, you can begin the process of reclaiming the beautiful qualities that made you a target:

- **Your Empathy** isn't a weakness—it's a superpower that allows you to connect deeply with others and sense what they need. In healthy relationships, your empathy will be treasured, not exploited.

- **Your Sense of Justice** isn't self-righteousness—it's integrity that the world desperately needs. Your ability to see unfairness and speak up about it makes you a natural advocate and leader.

- **Your Independence** isn't rebellion—it's strength that allows you to think for yourself and resist manipulation. Your autonomy is what will protect you from future toxic relationships.

- **Your Intelligence** isn't arrogance—it's perception that allows you to see through deception and understand complex situations. Your ability to think critically is a gift that will serve you throughout your life.

- **Your Authenticity** isn't being difficult—it's being real in a world full of facades. Your genuine self is what attracts healthy people and repels toxic ones.

- **Your Differences** aren't flaws—they're the unique gifts you bring to the world. Your individuality is what makes you irreplaceable and valuable.

These qualities that made you dangerous to your dysfunctional family will make you powerful in the healthy world. They're not character defects to be fixed—they're strengths to be celebrated and developed.

The Family's Real Problem

Your family's problem was never you. Their problem was their own dysfunction, their unhealed trauma, their emotional immaturity, and their inability to love authentically. They needed a scapegoat because they couldn't face their real issues.

They couldn't handle your emotional honesty because they were emotionally dishonest. They couldn't accept your moral clarity because they were morally confused. They couldn't tolerate your independence because they were psychologically dependent on control. They couldn't appreciate your authenticity because they were living lives built on lies.

You represented everything they couldn't be and were afraid to become. You were a mirror reflecting their potential for growth, and instead of using that reflection to heal, they tried to shatter the mirror.

Your selection as the scapegoat says nothing about your worth and everything about their limitations. You were chosen not because you were less than them, but because you were more than they could handle.

In the next chapter, we'll explore exactly what their inability to handle you did to your developing brain and nervous system. We'll look at the science behind how chronic stress and trauma literally rewired your brain to survive in their dysfunctional environment. Understanding this biological impact will help you see why healing feels so challenging and why your responses to stress and relationships might feel overwhelming sometimes.

But for now, I want you to sit with this truth: you were chosen because you were beautiful, not because you were broken. You were targeted because you were threatening their lies, not because you were living one. You were scapegoated because you were too healthy for their sick system, not because you were sick.

The very qualities that made them reject you are the qualities that make you valuable to the world. You weren't the problem then, and you're not the problem now. You were their solution that they were too broken to accept.

4

REWIRED FOR SURVIVAL

HOW CHRONIC TRAUMA CHANGED YOUR DEVELOPING BRAIN

U nderstanding that you were targeted for your positive qualities is just the beginning of your healing journey. Now we need to examine what that targeting actually did to you—not just emotionally or psychologically, but biologically. The systematic abuse you endured didn't just hurt your feelings or damage your self-esteem. It literally rewired your developing brain for survival in a hostile environment.

This isn't metaphorical language or therapeutic hyperbole. This is measurable, observable, scientifically documented change to your brain structure and function. The chronic stress of being the family scapegoat altered your neural pathways, your stress response systems, and your fundamental relationship with safety and threat.

Understanding this biological reality is crucial for several reasons. First, it validates that your struggles aren't character weaknesses or personal failings—they're normal adaptations to abnormal circumstances. Second, it explains why certain things feel so difficult for you as an adult, why relationships can feel overwhelming, and why your nervous system sometimes seems to have a mind of its own. Finally, it provides hope, because the same neuroplasticity that allowed trauma to change your brain can allow healing to change it back.

Your brain did exactly what it was supposed to do to keep you alive in an environment that wasn't safe. Now we need to help it understand that you're safe now and teach it new ways of being in the world.

Your Brain Under Siege

To understand what happened to your brain, you first need to understand what your brain was designed to do. The human brain is an incredible adaptation machine, constantly adjusting its structure and function based on the environment it finds itself in. This neuroplasticity—the brain's ability to rewire itself—is usually a tremendous advantage. It allows us to learn, grow, and adapt to new circumstances throughout our lives.

But when a child's brain develops in an environment of chronic stress, unpredictability, and emotional danger, this same plasticity becomes a survival mechanism that can create long-term challenges. Your brain adapted to keep you alive in your family environment, but those same adaptations can feel maladaptive when you're trying to live in healthier environments as an adult.

The Developing Brain in Trauma

During childhood and adolescence, your brain was still forming its fundamental neural pathways and structures. The experiences you had during this critical period literally shaped how your brain was wired. In a healthy environment, a child's brain develops with an expectation of safety, predictability, and responsive caregiving. In your environment, your brain developed with an expectation of danger, unpredictability, and threat.

Your brain had to make a crucial decision: develop optimally for learning and growth, or develop optimally for survival. In your family environment, survival won. Your brain allocated its resources toward threat detection, self-protection, and hypervigilance rather than toward exploration, curiosity, and secure attachment.

This wasn't a conscious choice, and it wasn't a mistake. Your brain was doing exactly what brains are designed to do—adapt to the environment to maximize survival. The problem is that survival-optimized brains can struggle in environments that are actually safe.

The Amygdala: Your Overactive Alarm System

The amygdala is a small, almond-shaped structure deep in your brain that serves as your threat detection system. In a healthy environment, the amygdala learns to distinguish between real dangers and normal life stressors. It sounds the alarm when there's genuine threat and stays quiet when you're safe.

In your family environment, the amygdala learned that danger could come at any time, often without warning. The criticism could start over anything. The blame could land on you regardless of your involvement. The emotional atmosphere could shift from calm to chaotic in an instant. Your amygdala learned to be constantly vigilant, always scanning for signs of incoming threat.

Hypervigilance: Always On Guard

This constant state of alertness is called hypervigilance, and it became your default mode. You learned to read facial expressions for the slightest sign of disapproval. You monitored tone of voice for hints of anger or irritation. You watched body language for signals that someone's mood was shifting.

You became expert at detecting micro-expressions, subtle changes in energy, and unspoken tension. You could walk into a room and immediately sense the emotional climate. You knew when someone was upset before they even realized it themselves.

While this hypervigilance helped protect you in your family environment, it's exhausting to maintain as an adult. Your nervous system never gets to fully relax because it's always scanning for potential threats. Even in safe environments, your amygdala may continue to sound false alarms, interpreting neutral situations as dangerous.

Hair-Trigger Responses

An overactive amygdala doesn't just detect more threats—it also reacts more intensely to them. Your fight-or-flight response may activate over situations that others would consider minor stressors. A critical comment from a supervisor might trigger the same physiological response that helped you survive your father's rages. A friend's cancellation of plans might activate the same abandonment panic that kept you hypervigilant to your mother's mood shifts.

This isn't overreacting or being too sensitive. This is your survival system responding to stimuli that resembles past threats, even when the current situation is objectively safe.

The Prefrontal Cortex: Your Overwhelmed CEO

While your amygdala was becoming hyperactive, another crucial part of your brain—the prefrontal cortex—was struggling to develop properly. The prefrontal cortex is often called the brain's CEO because it's responsible for executive functions like decision-making, impulse control, emotional regulation, and planning.

The prefrontal cortex is also the last part of the brain to fully develop, not reaching maturity until around age 25. This means it's particularly vulnerable to the effects of chronic stress during childhood and adolescence.

Impaired Executive Function

Chronic stress hormones like cortisol can actually impair the development of the prefrontal cortex, leading to difficulties with:

- **Decision-Making**: You might struggle with choices, big and small. Even simple decisions like what to eat for lunch can feel overwhelming. You might second-guess yourself constantly or freeze when faced with options.

- **Emotional Regulation:** Your emotions might feel intense and difficult to manage. You could go from calm to overwhelmed quickly, or feel emotions so intensely that they seem to take over your entire system.

- **Impulse Control:** You might struggle with saying things you later regret, making purchases you can't afford, or engaging in behaviors that you know aren't good for you.

- **Planning and Organization:** Long-term planning might feel impossible. You might struggle with following through on goals or maintaining organizational systems.

- **Working Memory:** You might have difficulty holding multiple pieces of information in your mind at once or struggle to concentrate when you're stressed.

These aren't character flaws or signs of laziness. These are the predictable results of a prefrontal cortex that developed under chronic stress.

The Hijacked Brain

When your amygdala perceives threat, it can essentially hijack your prefrontal cortex, taking you offline from your rational, thinking brain and putting you into pure survival mode. This is why you might find yourself reacting to situations in ways that don't make sense to you later.

In moments of activation, you might become someone you don't recognize—more defensive, more reactive, more emotional than feels authentic to who you are. This isn't you being weak or out of control. This is your survival brain taking over to protect you from what it perceives as danger.

The Hippocampus: Your Confused Librarian

The hippocampus is responsible for memory formation and processing. It's like your brain's librarian, filing away experiences and helping you make sense of what happened when. Chronic stress can significantly impact how the hippocampus functions, leading to problems with memory that many trauma survivors experience.

Fragmented Memories

Under chronic stress, the hippocampus may not properly encode memories, leading to fragmented or unclear recollections of your childhood. You might have:

- **Missing chunks of time** where you can't remember significant periods of your childhood

- **Vivid emotional memories** without clear details about what actually happened

- **Conflicting memories** where you remember the same event differently at different times

- **Intrusive memories** that pop up unexpectedly and feel overwhelming

- **Difficulty with chronology** where you can't place events in their proper timeline

This isn't evidence that you're imagining things or that the abuse wasn't serious. Fragmented memory is actually evidence of how overwhelmed your system was during those experiences.

Trauma Time

One of the most disorienting effects of hippocampal disruption is something called "trauma time." Past traumatic events can feel present and immediate, as if they're happening right now. This is why a criticism from your boss might not just remind you of your father's criticism—it might make you feel like you're actually back in childhood, experiencing that helplessness and terror all over again.

Your brain has difficulty distinguishing between past and present when it comes to trauma memories. The emotional and physical sensations can be just as intense as if the original event were happening right now.

The Stress Response System: Stuck in Overdrive

Your autonomic nervous system, which controls your body's automatic functions, has two main branches: the sympathetic nervous system (fight or flight) and the parasympathetic nervous system (rest and digest). In a healthy person, these systems work in balance, activating when needed and deactivating when the threat is over.

Chronic trauma can dysregulate this system, leaving you stuck in various states of activation or shutdown.

Hyperarousal: Fight or Flight Stuck On

You might experience chronic hyperarousal, where your sympathetic nervous system is constantly activated. This can feel like:

- **Constant anxiety or restlessness**

- **Difficulty sleeping or staying asleep**

- **Racing thoughts or mental chatter**

- **Physical tension or muscle pain**

- **Digestive issues**

- **Feeling jumpy or easily startled**

- **Difficulty concentrating**

You might feel like you're always "on," unable to fully relax even in safe environments.

Hypoarousal: The Shutdown Response

Alternatively, or sometimes in addition, you might experience hypoarousal, where your system shuts down to protect itself from overwhelming stress. This can feel like:

- **Emotional numbness or disconnection**

- **Feeling spaced out or dissociated**

- **Extreme fatigue or exhaustion**

- **Difficulty feeling emotions or physical sensations**

- **Feeling like you're watching your life from outside yourself**

- **Depression or hopelessness**

- **Window of Tolerance**

Healthy nervous systems have what's called a 'window of tolerance' — a term coined by psychiatrist Dr. Dan Siegel to describe the zone where you can experience stress and emotions without becoming overwhelmed or shutting down. Trauma often narrows this window significantly. Things that wouldn't bother most people might push you into hyperarousal or hypoarousal.

Your window of tolerance might be so narrow that normal life stresses—a difficult conversation, a busy day at work, even positive events like parties or celebrations—push you outside your zone of comfort and into dysregulation.

Complex PTSD: When Trauma Becomes Your Normal

While most people are familiar with PTSD as it relates to single traumatic events... the kind of trauma you experienced as a family scapegoat is different... This type of ongoing, relational trauma often leads to Complex PTSD (C-PTSD), a diagnosis officially recognized by the World Health Organization in the ICD-11 — though notably absent from the American DSM-5, which does not yet recognize it as a separate condition.

The Core Symptoms of Complex PTSD

- **Emotional Dysregulation**: Difficulty managing intense emotions, feeling overwhelmed by feelings, or conversely, feeling emotionally numb.

- **Negative Self-Concept**: Persistent feelings of worthlessness, shame, guilt, or being fundamentally flawed. This isn't just low self-esteem—it's a core belief that you are bad, wrong, or defective.

- **Interpersonal Difficulties**: Problems with maintaining healthy relationships, difficulty trusting others, fear of abandonment, or feeling fundamentally different from other people.

- **Attention and Consciousness Disruptions**: Dissociation, feeling spaced out, memory problems, or feeling disconnected from your body or surroundings.

- **Behavioral Control Issues**: Difficulty with impulse control, self-destructive behaviors, or compulsive behaviors.

- **Meaning-Making Disruptions**: Loss of faith, feeling hopeless about the future, or feeling like life has no meaning or purpose.

Why Complex PTSD Develops

C-PTSD typically develops when trauma occurs:

- **Repeatedly** over an extended period

- **During critical developmental periods** (childhood/adolescence)

- **In relationships** where the victim can't escape (family, caregiver relationships)

- **Where the perpetrator has power and control** over the victim

- **Without adequate support or intervention**

Your experience as a family scapegoat checks all these boxes. The abuse was ongoing, occurred during your developmental years, happened within your primary family relationships, was perpetrated by people who had complete power over you, and likely occurred without adequate outside support or protection.

The Body Keeps the Score

Trauma doesn't just affect your brain—it affects your entire body. Your body learned to be in a constant state of alert, and that chronic activation can lead to a wide range of physical symptoms and health issues.

Physical Symptoms of Chronic Trauma

- **Autoimmune Issues:** Chronic stress can dysregulate your immune system, leading to autoimmune conditions where your body attacks its own tissues.

- **Digestive Problems:** The gut is often called the "second brain" because it's so connected to your nervous system. Chronic stress can lead to IBS, chronic stomach pain, food sensitivities, or other digestive issues.

- **Chronic Pain:** Muscle tension from chronic hypervigilance can lead to chronic headaches, back pain, neck pain, or fibromyalgia.

- **Sleep Disorders:** Difficulty falling asleep, staying asleep, or getting restorative sleep.

- **Cardiovascular Issues:** Chronic stress puts strain on your heart and circulatory system.

- **Hormonal Imbalances:** Stress can disrupt your endocrine system, affecting everything from your menstrual cycle to your thyroid function.

Somatic Memories

Your body also stores memories of trauma in ways that your conscious mind might not be able to access. You might have physical reactions—tension, pain, nausea, panic—in response to situations that remind your body of past trauma, even when your mind doesn't make the connection.

A certain tone of voice might make your shoulders tense. A particular facial expression might make your stomach clench. A specific type of conflict might make your chest feel tight. These aren't overreactions—these are your body's memories trying to protect you.

Emotional Suppression: Shutting Down to Survive

One of the most common adaptations scapegoated children make is learning to suppress their emotions. In your family environment, expressing authentic emotions was often punished, dismissed, or used against you. Your brain learned that emotions were dangerous and developed sophisticated mechanisms to shut them down.

Why You Learned to Suppress

You didn't suppress your emotions because you were weak or "too sensitive." You did it because your environment demanded it. Over time, shutting down became the safer option—sometimes the only option.

- **Self-Preservation**: Whenever you reacted honestly, the abuse escalated. So you learned to quiet yourself, to disappear emotionally, because staying small felt safer than provoking another explosion.

- **Fear of Consequences**: Anger, sadness, fear—any real feeling—often came with criticism, punishment, or labels meant to shame you into silence. It didn't take long to learn that expressing anything real had a cost.

- **Gaslighting and Doubt**: When your feelings were denied, mocked, or twisted, you began questioning your own emotional reality. Suppression became easier than constantly wondering whether you were "wrong."

- **Survival Mode:** When you're living in a state of threat, there's no bandwidth for reflection or emotional processing. Everything gets pushed down, numbed out, or buried so you can make it through the moment.

You adapted to stay alive—emotionally, sometimes physically. Suppression wasn't a flaw. It was a survival skill

The Eight Ways You Learned to Suppress

You didn't wake up one day and decide to push your emotions down. You learned to do it because your environment taught you these strategies were safer than feeling the full truth of your experience. They show up in all kinds of familiar ways:

- **Dissociation:** You drift out of your body or your surroundings when things get overwhelming, almost like your mind hits an emergency exit.

- **Hypervigilance:** You're so busy scanning for danger or reading the room that there's no space left to notice what's happening inside you.

- **Perfectionism:** You keep yourself endlessly occupied trying to get everything right, which conveniently leaves no room to feel anything uncomfortable.

- **People-Pleasing:** You pour your attention into what everyone else needs or feels, leaving your own emotions on the back burner—or off the stove completely.

- **Addiction or Compulsive Behaviors:** Whether it's food, work, shopping, substances, or scrolling, the pull is the same: anything that helps you numb out or create distance from what's really going on.

- **Intellectualization:** You stay in analysis mode, turning everything into a thought problem. Thinking becomes a shield so you don't have to feel.

- **Minimization:** You tell yourself your emotions don't matter or aren't worth the attention. You downplay your experience before anyone else can.

- **Physical Suppression:** Your body holds what your mind won't. Tight muscles, shallow breaths, clenched jaws—your physical patterns become the container for emotions you never felt safe expressing.

These patterns didn't appear out of nowhere. They were survival strategies long before they became habits.

The Cost of Suppression

While emotional suppression helped you survive your childhood, it comes with significant costs:

- **Disconnection from Yourself:** When you shut down difficult emotions, you often shut down positive emotions too. You might feel numb, empty, or like you're going through the motions of life.

- **Difficulty with Intimacy:** Healthy relationships require emotional vulnerability and authenticity. Suppression makes it difficult to connect deeply with others.

- **Accumulation of Emotional Pressure:** Suppressed emotions don't disappear—they build up pressure. You might experience sudden emotional outbursts or feel overwhelmed when emotions finally surface.

- **Physical Health Issues:** Suppressed emotions often get stored in the body, contributing to chronic pain, tension, and health problems.

- **Loss of Inner Guidance:** Emotions provide important information about your needs, boundaries, and values. Suppression cuts you off from this internal wisdom.

The Positive Side of Your Adaptations

While understanding the damage is important, it's equally important to recognize that your brain's adaptations weren't just problems—they were also incredible feats of survival and resilience.

Your hypervigilance made you incredibly perceptive and empathetic. Your ability to read people and situations is a superpower that serves you well in healthy relationships and professional settings.

Your threat detection system, while sometimes overactive, also keeps you safe from genuinely dangerous people and situations. You can spot manipulation, deception, and toxicity quickly because your brain is trained to detect these patterns.

Your emotional suppression, while costly, also gave you incredible strength and resilience. You survived situations that might have broken others because you could function even under extreme stress.

Your independence and self-reliance, born from not being able to depend on your family, made you incredibly capable and resourceful.

These adaptations aren't just wounds to be healed—they're also strengths to be appreciated and channeled in healthy directions.

Neuroplasticity: Your Brain's Capacity for Healing

Here's the most important thing I want you to understand: the same neuroplasticity that allowed trauma to rewire your brain also allows healing to rewire it back toward health.

Your brain isn't permanently damaged or broken. It's adapted. And just as it adapted to survive trauma, it can adapt to thrive in safety.

How Healing Changes Your Brain

Healing rewires the very systems that once shut down under stress, allowing your brain to regain clarity, balance, and emotional freedom.

- **Therapy and Safe Relationships**: Working with trauma-informed therapists and building safe, healthy relationships literally rewires your brain for connection and trust.

- **Mindfulness and Meditation**: These practices strengthen your prefrontal cortex and help regulate your amygdala, increasing your window of tolerance.

- **Body-Based Practices**: Yoga, massage, movement therapy, and other somatic approaches help your nervous system learn to settle and regulate.

- **EMDR and Trauma Processing**: Specific trauma therapies help your hippocampus properly process and file away traumatic memories.

- **Safe Emotional Expression**: Learning to feel and express emotions safely helps restore your natural emotional regulation systems.

- **Corrective Experiences**: Each positive relationship interaction, each moment of genuine safety, each experience of being valued and respected helps your brain update its threat assessment systems.

The Timeline of Healing

Neuroplastic change doesn't happen overnight, but it does happen. Neuroscience researchers Richard Davidson and Bruce McEwen have found that significant changes can begin within weeks of starting trauma-informed treatment, with continued improvement over months and years.

Your brain is incredibly resilient and wants to heal. With the right support, environment, and practices, you can teach your nervous system that you're safe now, that emotions are safe to feel, that relationships can be trustworthy, and that you deserve care and respect.

The child who was forced to adapt to survive in a hostile environment can become the adult who thrives in a safe one. Your brain has been waiting your entire life for the safety to heal. Now that you understand what happened and why, you can begin to provide that safety for yourself.

In the next chapter, we'll explore how to reconnect with the emotions you learned to suppress and begin the process of emotional integration that's essential for healing. But for now, I want you to appreciate the incredible resilience and adaptability of the brain that kept you alive and brought you to this moment of understanding.

You survived something that could have destroyed you. Your brain did exactly what it needed to do to keep you alive. Now it's time to help it learn to live.

Part II: Understanding the Madness

Creative Media Enterprises

5

THE EMOTIONAL WASTELAND

HOW YOU LEARNED TO SURVIVE BY SHUTTING DOWN

If you're like most family scapegoats, you learned early that emotions were dangerous territory. Your natural emotional responses to unfairness, abuse, and neglect were consistently met with punishment, dismissal, or escalation of the very treatment that caused them in the first place. So you did what any intelligent child would do: you learned to shut them down.

This emotional suppression wasn't a conscious choice—it was a survival adaptation. Your developing brain made a calculation that feeling less was safer than feeling authentically. In your family environment, this calculation was probably correct. Emotions made you vulnerable to attack, gave your abusers ammunition to use against you, and often made terrible situations even worse.

But now, as an adult trying to heal and build healthy relationships, this same protective mechanism has become a barrier to the very connection and authenticity you long for. You may find yourself feeling numb when you want to feel joy, disconnected when you want intimacy, or overwhelmed when emotions finally surface after years of suppression.

Understanding how you learned to suppress emotions—and why it was necessary—is crucial for learning to feel safely again. This isn't about judging your survival mechanisms or rushing to dismantle them. It's about appreciating how brilliantly your psyche protected you and then gently teaching it that it's safe to feel again.

Why Your Brain Chose Suppression

Emotional suppression in traumatic environments isn't a character flaw or a sign of weakness—it's an intelligent adaptation to impossible circumstances. Your brain had to choose between optimal emotional development and immediate survival, and survival won.

Emotions Made You a Target

In healthy families, children's emotions are welcomed, validated, and used as information about their needs and experiences. In your family, emotions made you vulnerable to increased abuse.

If you cried when criticized, you were told you were "too sensitive" or "playing the victim." If you expressed anger at unfair treatment, you were labeled "disrespectful" or "out of control." If you showed fear or anxiety, you were either dismissed as "dramatic" or your fear was used to manipulate and control you further.

Your authentic emotional responses threatened the family's carefully maintained narrative that everything was fine and you were the problem. They needed you to accept abuse quietly, to minimize your own pain, and to prioritize their comfort over your emotional truth.

Emotions Were Weaponized Against You

Not only were your emotions dismissed, they were often turned into weapons to use against you. If you expressed sadness about mistreatment, it was used as evidence that you were "mentally unstable" or "always playing the victim." If you showed excitement about an achievement, it was labeled as "showing off" or "thinking you're better than everyone."

Your vulnerabilities were catalogued and stored for future use. If they knew you were sensitive about your appearance, that became a regular target for criticism. If they knew you cared deeply about animals, threats to pets became a control mechanism. Your emotional landscape became a map of potential attack points.

There Was No Safe Space to Process

Healthy emotional development requires safe spaces where children can express feelings without fear of retaliation. You had no such space. Home wasn't safe because that's where the abuse was happening. Extended family often either didn't know about the abuse or were part of the enabling system. School provided temporary relief but wasn't equipped to handle complex family trauma.

Without a safe space to feel and process emotions, your brain decided the safest option was to stop feeling as much as possible. If you couldn't process emotions safely, the next best option was to minimize them.

Survival Required All Your Resources

Living in a state of chronic stress and hypervigilance requires enormous mental and emotional resources. Your brain had to allocate energy toward threat detection, emotional regulation to avoid triggering abusers, and constant strategic thinking about how to navigate each day safely.

There simply weren't enough resources left over for the full emotional processing that healthy development requires. Your brain prioritized immediate survival over emotional development, knowing it could address the emotional backlog later if you survived to adulthood.

The Eight Ways You Learned to Suppress

Understanding how you learned to suppress emotions helps you recognize these patterns in your adult life and begin to gently work with them rather than against them.

Dissociation: Leaving Your Body Behind

Dissociation is perhaps the most common emotional suppression strategy among trauma survivors. It's the ability to mentally disconnect from your body and emotions when situations become overwhelming.

You might have learned to "float above" yourself during abuse, watching what was happening as if it were a movie rather than your real life. You might have developed the ability to "check out" mentally during criticism or conflict, appearing present while actually being mentally absent.

As an adult, you might find yourself dissociating during conflict, medical procedures, intimacy, or any situation that feels overwhelming. You might feel "spaced out," like you're watching your life from outside yourself, or like you're not fully present in your own experiences.

Dissociation served you well during trauma, but it can interfere with your ability to feel emotions, connect with others, or be fully present in positive experiences.

Hypervigilance: Staying Focused on External Threats

When all your attention is focused on scanning for external threats, there's no attention left for internal emotional experiences. Hypervigilance can be an extremely effective way to suppress emotions because it keeps your entire nervous system focused outward.

You might have become an expert at reading the emotional climate of every room you entered, monitoring facial expressions for signs of anger or disapproval, or staying constantly alert to potential criticism or conflict.

As an adult, you might find that you're so focused on other people's emotions and reactions that you have no idea what you're feeling. You might be able to sense when someone else is upset before they know it themselves, but be completely disconnected from your own emotional state.

Perfectionism: Staying Too Busy to Feel

Perfectionism can be an effective emotional suppression strategy because it keeps you so focused on external performance that there's no time or energy left for internal emotional processing.

You might have learned that perfect behavior could sometimes protect you from abuse, or at least minimize it. Even when perfection didn't prevent mistreatment, it became a way to stay focused on controllable external factors rather than uncontrollable emotional pain.

As an adult, you might find yourself driven to achieve, constantly busy with projects and goals, or unable to rest because stopping would mean feeling. You might have learned to derive your sense of worth entirely from external achievements rather than internal emotional experiences.

People-Pleasing: Focusing on Others' Emotions

When you become an expert at managing other people's emotions and needs, you can effectively avoid dealing with your own. People-pleasing involves becoming so attuned to others' emotional states that you lose track of your own.

You might have learned that keeping everyone else happy was the best way to stay safe. If you could anticipate and meet others' needs before they even expressed them, you might be able to avoid triggering their anger or disappointment.

As an adult, you might find that you know immediately when someone else is upset but have no idea how you feel about a situation. You might be an expert at providing emotional support to others while feeling completely disconnected from your own emotional needs.

Intellectualization: Living in Your Head

Intellectualization involves moving emotional experiences entirely into the realm of thoughts and analysis. Instead of feeling emotions, you think about them, analyze them, and try to understand them logically.

You might have learned that thinking about problems was safer than feeling them. Emotions felt dangerous and unpredictable, but thoughts felt controllable and manageable.

As an adult, you might be able to analyze your childhood and understand intellectually that you were abused, but struggle to feel the anger, sadness, or grief that would be natural responses to that understanding. You might relate to your life as a series of events to be understood rather than experiences to be felt.

Minimization: Making Everything Smaller

Minimization involves consistently downplaying the significance of both events and your emotional responses to them. It's a way of suppressing emotions by convincing yourself they're not justified or important.

You might have learned that making your pain smaller made it more bearable and less likely to trigger additional abuse. If you could convince yourself that the mistreatment "wasn't that bad," you didn't have to feel the full impact of how much it hurt.

As an adult, you might automatically minimize positive achievements ("It was no big deal") and traumatic experiences ("Other people have it worse"). You might struggle to feel the full impact of both good and bad experiences because you've learned to make everything emotionally smaller.

Addictive or Compulsive Behaviors: Numbing the Pain

Addictive and compulsive behaviors can be effective ways to suppress emotions by providing temporary relief from emotional pain or creating different neurochemical states that override natural emotions.

You might have learned to use food, substances, work, shopping, relationships, or other behaviors to change your internal state when emotions became overwhelming.

As an adult, you might find yourself reaching for these behaviors automatically when emotions surface, or you might structure your entire life around activities that prevent you from having quiet time when emotions might emerge.

Physical Suppression: Holding It in Your Body

Emotions are physical experiences, and they can be suppressed through physical mechanisms like shallow breathing, muscle tension, or other ways of literally holding feelings in your body.

You might have learned to hold your breath when scared, tense your shoulders when angry, or clench your jaw when sad. These physical patterns can effectively prevent emotions from being fully felt or expressed.

As an adult, you might carry chronic tension in your body, struggle with breathing deeply, or find that emotions feel "stuck" or difficult to access. Your body might have become a storage container for unexpressed emotions.

The Hidden Costs of Suppression

While emotional suppression served a crucial protective function during your traumatic childhood, it comes with significant costs that become more apparent as you try to build healthy adult relationships and authentic life experiences.

Emotional Numbness and Disconnection

When you shut down difficult emotions, you often shut down positive emotions as well. The same mechanisms that protect you from feeling pain also prevent you from feeling joy, excitement, love, and satisfaction.

You might feel like you're going through the motions of life without really experiencing it. Accomplishments might feel hollow, relationships might feel distant, and experiences that should be meaningful might feel flat or empty.

This numbness isn't depression, though it can feel similar. It's the predictable result of a nervous system that learned to turn down emotional volume to survive.

Difficulty with Intimacy and Connection

Healthy relationships require emotional vulnerability and authenticity. When you've learned to suppress emotions for safety, intimacy can feel terrifying because it requires the very emotional openness that once made you vulnerable to attack.

You might find yourself pushing people away when they get too close, sabotaging relationships when they become meaningful, or feeling anxious and overwhelmed by the emotional demands of intimate connection.

You might also struggle with knowing what you actually want or need in relationships because you've been so focused on what's safe rather than what's authentic.

Accumulation of Emotional Pressure

Suppressed emotions don't disappear—they accumulate. Over time, this can create enormous internal pressure that eventually needs release.

You might experience sudden emotional outbursts that seem disproportionate to the triggering event. You might have periods of intense depression, anxiety, or anger that feel like they come out of nowhere. You might find that small stressors trigger overwhelming emotional responses because they're tapping into years of accumulated unexpressed emotion.

Loss of Internal Guidance

Emotions provide crucial information about your needs, values, boundaries, and preferences. When you suppress emotions, you lose access to this internal guidance system.

You might struggle with decision-making because you can't access your true preferences. You might have difficulty setting boundaries because you can't feel when they're being violated. You might find yourself in situations or relationships that aren't good for you because you can't feel the warning signals your emotions would normally provide.

Physical Health Consequences

Suppressed emotions often get stored in the body, contributing to chronic pain, tension, autoimmune issues, digestive problems, and other physical health challenges.

Your body becomes a storage container for unexpressed emotions, and over time, this can create significant physical symptoms and health problems.

Increased Vulnerability to Manipulation

When you're disconnected from your own emotions, you become more vulnerable to manipulation by others who may not have your best interests at heart.

You might find yourself in relationships with people who exploit your emotional numbness, or you might struggle to recognize when people are trying to manipulate or control you because you can't access your internal warning systems.

Coping Mechanisms: Survival Strategies That Became Habits

In addition to emotional suppression, you likely developed other coping mechanisms to survive your traumatic family environment.

Understanding these patterns helps you recognize them in your adult life and work with them consciously rather than being controlled by them unconsciously.

Hypervigilance and People-Reading

You became an expert at reading people's emotional states, facial expressions, and body language to predict potential threats. This hypervigilance helped keep you safe but can be exhausting to maintain as an adult.

You might find yourself constantly monitoring other people's moods, feeling responsible for managing their emotions, or feeling anxious when you can't read someone's emotional state clearly.

Fawn Response: Appeasing to Survive

The fawn response involves appeasing potential threats through excessive compliance, people-pleasing, and self-sacrifice. If you couldn't fight back or run away, making yourself useful and non-threatening became a survival strategy.

As an adult, you might automatically prioritize other people's needs over your own, struggle to say no to requests, or find yourself in relationships where you give much more than you receive.

Control and Predictability Seeking

In chaotic, unpredictable family environments, you might have tried to create safety through control and predictability wherever possible.

As an adult, you might struggle with flexibility, feel anxious when plans change, or try to control situations and people in ways that interfere with natural relationship dynamics.

Achievement and Performance

You might have learned that achievement could sometimes protect you from abuse or earn you temporary positive attention. Excellence became a survival strategy.

As an adult, you might be driven to achieve but struggle to enjoy your accomplishments, feel like you're never good enough regardless of your success, or derive your entire sense of worth from external achievements.

Isolation and Self-Reliance

When other people consistently hurt or disappointed you, self-reliance became the safest option. You learned that depending on yourself was more reliable than depending on others.

As an adult, you might struggle to ask for help, feel uncomfortable with vulnerability, or have difficulty accepting support from others even when it's freely offered.

Minimization and Denial

Making your own pain smaller helped you survive it. Convincing yourself that abuse "wasn't that bad" or that you "deserved it" might have felt better than acknowledging the full extent of the betrayal and harm.

As an adult, you might automatically minimize both positive and negative experiences, struggle to acknowledge the severity of past trauma, or have difficulty celebrating achievements and recognizing your own worth.

The Wisdom of Your Adaptations

Before we talk about healing and change, it's important to acknowledge the wisdom and intelligence of your survival adaptations. These weren't random or pathological responses—they were brilliant solutions to impossible problems.

Your emotional suppression kept you alive. Your hypervigilance protected you from additional harm. Your people-pleasing minimized dangerous conflict. Your perfectionism sometimes earned you temporary safety. Your self-reliance protected you from the pain of repeated disappointment.

These adaptations demonstrate remarkable resilience, intelligence, and survival instinct. They're evidence of your strength, not your weakness.

The goal of healing isn't to judge these adaptations or get rid of them entirely. Some of them will continue to serve you throughout your life. The goal is to develop choice about when and how you use them, so they become tools you can consciously employ rather than automatic patterns that control you.

From Survival to Thriving

The nervous system that adapted for survival in trauma can learn to adapt for thriving in safety. Your brain that learned to suppress emotions for protection can learn to feel safely in supportive environments.

This doesn't mean forcing yourself to feel everything all at once or dismantling your protective mechanisms before you've developed healthier alternatives. It means gradually, gently teaching your nervous system that some environments are safe for authentic emotional expression.

Recognizing Suppression in Your Adult Life

Understanding how emotional suppression shows up in your adult life is the first step toward working with it consciously rather than being controlled by it unconsciously.

Signs You May Still Be Suppressing

- **Emotional Numbness**: Feeling flat, empty, or like you're going through the motions of life without really experiencing it.

- **Difficulty Identifying Emotions**: Not knowing what you're feeling in the moment, or only being able to identify emotions as "good" or "bad" rather than specifically.

- **Physical Symptoms:** Chronic tension, headaches, digestive issues, or other physical symptoms that don't have clear medical causes.

- **Relationship Difficulties:** Struggling with intimacy, feeling disconnected from partners, or having relationships that feel superficial.

- **Sudden Emotional Outbursts:** Having emotional reactions that feel disproportionate to the triggering event.

- **Difficulty with Positive Emotions:** Struggling to feel joy, excitement, or satisfaction even during positive experiences.

- **Hypervigilance:** Constantly monitoring other people's emotions while being disconnected from your own.

- **Decision-Making Difficulties:** Struggling to make choices because you can't access your preferences or feelings about options.

The Paradox of Safety

One of the most confusing aspects of emotional suppression is that it often increases when you're actually safer. Your nervous system might have learned to suppress emotions so completely that it continues doing so even in safe, supportive environments.

You might find that you feel more emotional numbness in your healthy relationship than you did in toxic ones. You might struggle more with emotional expression when you're in therapy than when you were in crisis. This isn't a sign that you're going backward—it's a sign that your nervous system is finally safe enough to maintain the protective mechanisms that kept you alive.

The Path Back to Feeling

Learning to feel safely again is a gradual process that requires patience, self-compassion, and often professional support. It's not about forcing emotions to surface or demanding that your nervous system change immediately. It's about creating conditions where authentic emotional expression becomes possible.

Building Emotional Safety

Before you can access suppressed emotions, you need to create internal and external safety for emotional expression.

Internal Safety: This means developing a compassionate relationship with yourself where all emotions are welcome, even difficult ones. It means learning to tolerate emotional intensity without judgment or panic.

External Safety: This means surrounding yourself with people who can handle your authentic emotions without trying to fix, change, or judge them. It means creating physical spaces where you feel safe to feel.

Starting Small

Emotional reconnection often begins with small, manageable experiences rather than dramatic emotional releases.

You might start by noticing physical sensations in your body rather than trying to identify complex emotions. You might practice naming simple emotions in low-stakes situations before attempting to process traumatic material.

Working with the Body

Since emotions are physical experiences, body-based approaches are often essential for emotional reconnection.

Practices like yoga, massage, breathwork, or somatic therapy can help your nervous system learn to feel sensations and emotions safely. These approaches work with your body's wisdom rather than trying to override it with cognitive understanding.

Professional Support

Reconnecting with suppressed emotions, especially those related to trauma, often requires skilled professional support. Trauma-informed therapists can help you navigate this process safely and at an appropriate pace.

Working with someone who understands the function and wisdom of emotional suppression can help you honor your protective mechanisms while gradually expanding your capacity for authentic emotional expression.

In the next chapter, we'll explore the specific ways that growing up in your family environment affected your development and how those effects show up in your adult life. Understanding these impacts will help you see that your struggles aren't character flaws but predictable responses to abnormal treatment.

But for now, I want you to appreciate the incredible intelligence of the emotional suppression that kept you alive. Your ability to survive by shutting down was a remarkable adaptation to impossible circumstances. Now that you're safer, you can begin the gentle process of teaching your nervous system that it's safe to feel again.

The emotions you learned to suppress are still there, waiting for you when you're ready. They're not gone—they're protected. And when you're ready, they'll be there to guide you back to your authentic self.

6

THE THREE PILLARS OF DESTRUCTION

HOW NARCISSISTIC PARENTS SYSTEMATICALLY DAMAGE THEIR CHILDREN

Now that you understand what happened to your brain and emotions, we need to examine the specific mechanisms your narcissistic family used to damage your development. This wasn't random cruelty or simple neglect. It was systematic psychological warfare conducted through three primary methods that work together to devastate a child's sense of self, safety, and worth.

These three pillars of destruction—identity attacks, boundary violations, and emotional parentification—form the foundation of how narcissistic parents break down their children's natural psychological development. Years of working with survivors reveals these patterns emerge consistently across different families and circumstances, suggesting a systematic approach to maintaining control through psychological domination.

Understanding these mechanisms helps explain why your struggles feel so fundamental, why healing can feel so challenging, and why the damage goes so much deeper than simple "bad parenting."

Each of these methods serves a specific function in maintaining the narcissistic parent's control while systematically undermining the child's healthy development. They work synergistically, each one reinforcing the others to create a comprehensive system of psychological domination.

The First Pillar: Identity Attacks

Your narcissistic parent didn't just criticize your behavior—they attacked your fundamental sense of who you are. This wasn't occasional harshness or frustration with specific actions. Clinical observations reveal this as deliberate, systematic assault on your core identity, designed to make you doubt your own worth, perceptions, and right to exist as a separate person.

Character Assassination vs. Behavioral Correction

Healthy parents correct behavior while preserving the child's sense of fundamental worth. They might say, "Please clean your room" or "That behavior isn't acceptable." The message is clear: your actions need to change, but you as a person are still valued and loved.

Your narcissistic parent did the opposite. Instead of addressing specific behaviors, they attacked your character. You didn't just make a mistake—you were "stupid." You didn't just act selfishly—you were "a selfish person." You didn't just have a bad day—you were "impossible to deal with."

These character attacks served multiple purposes. They deflected attention from the parent's own behavior by making you the problem. They prevented you from developing a stable, positive sense of self. Most importantly, they made you question your own perceptions and reality.

When someone tells you that you're "too sensitive" or "always causing drama," they're not just dismissing your current feelings—they're telling you that your emotional reactions are fundamentally flawed. Over time, you learn to distrust your own emotional responses and rely on others to tell you what's real.

The Labeling Trap

Narcissistic parents excel at applying negative labels that become self-fulfilling prophecies. Recovery work consistently shows how these labels become psychological prisons. Once you were labeled as "the difficult one," "the problem child," or "the sensitive one," every subsequent interaction got filtered through that lens.

If the "difficult" child had a normal emotional reaction to unfair treatment, it was evidence of how difficult they were. If the "sensitive" child cried when hurt, it proved they were too sensitive rather than revealing that they had been genuinely harmed.

These labels became prisons that were almost impossible to escape. No matter how you behaved, the label provided a framework for interpreting your actions negatively. Good behavior was dismissed as temporary or fake. Bad behavior was evidence that the label was accurate.

The labels also became part of how you saw yourself. After years of being told you were selfish, difficult, or dramatic, you internalized these descriptions as truth. Even when you succeeded or behaved well, part of you believed it was just a matter of time before your "true nature" emerged.

Gaslighting: Rewriting Your Reality

Perhaps the most devastating identity attack was the systematic gaslighting that made you question your own perceptions, memories, and sanity. Your narcissistic parent didn't just disagree with your version of events—they convinced you that your version was fundamentally flawed.

"That never happened." "You're remembering it wrong." "You're being too sensitive." "You're imagining things." These phrases weren't just dismissals—they were attacks on your basic ability to perceive and interpret reality accurately.

Survivors consistently describe how this gaslighting created profound self-doubt that extended far beyond their relationship with their parent. You learned to question your own memories, doubt your emotional reactions, and seek external validation for your perceptions of reality.

This self-doubt became a permanent feature of your psychological landscape. Even as an adult, you might find yourself questioning whether your memories are accurate, whether your emotional reactions are appropriate, or whether you can trust your own judgment about people and situations.

The Invisible Child

Some narcissistic parents attacked identity through complete dismissal and emotional neglect. If you were the lost child, your identity was attacked not through active criticism but through systematic invisibility.

Your thoughts, feelings, needs, and preferences were consistently ignored or dismissed as unimportant. You learned that who you were fundamentally didn't matter to the people who were supposed to love you most.

This creates a particular kind of identity damage where you don't develop a strong sense of self because no one ever reflected back to you that you were worth knowing. You became expert at disappearing, at making yourself small, at not taking up space or requiring attention.

Clinical experience shows this invisibility can be as damaging as active abuse because it prevents the development of a coherent sense of self. When no one sees you, validates you, or responds to your authentic self, you begin to question whether that authentic self has any value or even exists.

The Second Pillar: Boundary Violations

Healthy development requires clear, consistent boundaries that help children understand where they end and others begin. Your narcissistic parent systematically violated these boundaries, creating confusion about your right to autonomy, privacy, and self-determination.

Recovery work reveals that boundary violations often feel more subtle than other forms of abuse, making them harder to recognize and address. Yet they form a crucial foundation for the systematic control that characterizes narcissistic family systems.

Physical Boundary Violations

Your body wasn't treated as your own. Privacy was invaded through room searches, diary reading, or forced physical affection. Your belongings weren't really yours—they could be taken, destroyed, or given away without your consent.

Physical boundaries teach children that they have a right to bodily autonomy and personal space. When these boundaries are consistently violated, children learn that their physical selves are not under their own control.

You might have been forced to hug or kiss relatives when you were uncomfortable. Your room might have been searched without permission. Your personal items might have been taken or destroyed as punishment. Your physical privacy might have been invaded in ways that felt shameful or confusing.

These violations taught you that your comfort, consent, and physical autonomy were less important than other people's desires or convenience. You learned to override your own physical discomfort to please others, setting the stage for future relationships where your boundaries might be violated.

Emotional Boundary Violations

Your emotions were not treated as your own. Your narcissistic parent might have told you how you should feel, dismissed your authentic emotions as wrong or inappropriate, or used your emotions to manipulate and control you.

Healthy emotional boundaries allow children to have their own feelings without being responsible for managing their parents' emotions. Your boundaries were violated when you were made responsible for your parent's emotional state or when your emotions were treated as inconvenient problems to be eliminated.

You might have been told not to be sad because it made your parent feel bad. You might have been punished for expressing anger because it threatened your parent's authority. You might have been made to feel guilty for being happy when your parent was struggling.

These violations taught you that your emotions existed to serve others rather than to provide information about your own needs and experiences. You learned to monitor and manage other people's emotions while disconnecting from your own.

Mental and Psychological Boundary Violations

Your thoughts, opinions, and inner world were not treated as separate from your parent's. Your narcissistic parent might have insisted they knew what you were thinking, told you what your motivations were, or punished you for mental or emotional experiences you had no control over.

Healthy psychological boundaries allow children to have private thoughts, develop their own opinions, and maintain an inner life that belongs to them alone. Your boundaries were violated when your parent claimed to know your thoughts, motivations, or feelings better than you did.

You might have been told that you didn't really feel what you said you felt. Your motivations might have been consistently misinterpreted in the most negative possible light. Your private thoughts might have been treated as evidence of your character flaws.

These violations prevented you from developing a clear sense of your own mental and emotional autonomy. You learned that your inner world was not private or safe, and that others had the right to interpret your internal experiences for you.

The Parentification Trap

One of the most damaging boundary violations was parentification—being forced to take on adult responsibilities and emotional burdens that were inappropriate for your developmental stage. What emerges consistently in survivor accounts is how this role reversal fundamentally alters a child's understanding of relationships and responsibility.

You might have been made responsible for managing family conflicts, caring for younger siblings, or providing emotional support to your troubled parent. These responsibilities blurred the appropriate boundaries between parent and child, forcing you to develop capabilities you weren't ready for while missing out on the protection and care you needed.

Parentification teaches children that their needs are less important than adult needs and that their role is to serve others rather than to be cared for. It creates premature independence that looks like strength but is actually a trauma response to inadequate care.

As an adult, you might struggle with accepting help, feel uncomfortable with vulnerability, or automatically assume responsibility for managing other people's problems and emotions. You might feel guilty when you're not helping others or find it difficult to prioritize your own needs.

The Third Pillar: Emotional Parentification

The third pillar of systematic damage was emotional parentification—forcing you to manage the emotional needs and well-being of adults while your own emotional development was ignored or actively hindered. This represents perhaps the most insidious form of psychological abuse because it masquerades as closeness or trust while actually serving the parent's emotional needs at the child's expense.

Becoming the Family Therapist

Many scapegoated children are forced into the role of family emotional manager. You might have been expected to mediate conflicts between your parents, provide emotional support during their crises, or serve as a confidant for adult problems that were inappropriate for a child to handle.

This role reversal is profoundly damaging because it prevents children from developing their own emotional regulation skills while burdening them with emotional responsibilities they're not equipped to handle. Clinical observations show that children in this role often develop hypervigilance to others' emotional states while becoming disconnected from their own emotional experiences.

You learned that your value came from your ability to manage other people's emotions and solve their problems. Your own emotional needs became secondary to your function as the family's emotional caretaker.

The psychological burden of being responsible for adult emotions while still being a child creates lasting confusion about appropriate relationship dynamics and personal responsibility.

The Emotional Dumping Ground

Your narcissistic parent might have used you as an emotional dumping ground, sharing their frustrations, fears, and problems without regard for the impact on your development. You became their therapist, their emotional support system, their confidant—roles that should have been filled by other adults.

Survivor experiences reveal how this emotional dumping taught them that relationships were primarily about managing other people's emotions rather than mutual care and support. You learned to be hyperattuned to others' emotional needs while remaining disconnected from your own.

This dynamic also taught you that love means absorbing other people's pain and that your value in relationships comes from your utility as an emotional processor rather than from your inherent worth as a person.

Emotional Incest

In some cases, the emotional parentification crosses into what therapists call "emotional incest"—when a parent treats a child as an emotional partner or spouse substitute. This might involve sharing inappropriate details about marriage problems, using the child as primary emotional support, or creating an inappropriately intimate emotional bond.

This dynamic teaches children that love is conditional on meeting adult emotional needs and that healthy boundaries are selfish or hurtful. It creates confusion about appropriate relationship dynamics that can persist throughout life.

The emotional intensity of these relationships can feel like love or special connection, making them particularly difficult to recognize as abusive. Many survivors describe feeling both special and burdened by their role as their parent's emotional confidant.

Suppression of Your Emotional Development

While you were forced to manage everyone else's emotions, your own emotional development was not just neglected—it was actively suppressed. Your emotions were treated as inconvenient, inappropriate, or dangerous.

You learned that your role was to absorb other people's emotional pain without adding any of your own. Your feelings became burdens that made other people's lives more difficult rather than important information about your own needs and experiences.

Recovery work consistently reveals how this suppression created a fundamental disconnect from their own emotional life that can take years to heal. You might struggle to identify your own emotions, feel guilty for having needs, or find it difficult to prioritize your own emotional well-being.

How the Three Pillars Work Together

These three forms of systematic damage—identity attacks, boundary violations, and emotional parentification—don't work in isolation. They reinforce each other to create a comprehensive system of psychological control and developmental disruption. Understanding their interconnected nature helps explain why the damage feels so pervasive and why healing requires addressing multiple areas simultaneously.

Identity Attacks Enable Boundary Violations

When you're convinced that you're fundamentally flawed, you're less likely to protect your boundaries. If you believe you're "too sensitive," you won't trust your discomfort when boundaries are violated. If you think you're "selfish," you'll feel guilty for wanting privacy or autonomy.

The identity attacks create a psychological framework where boundary violations feel deserved or necessary. You learn to override your own discomfort because you've been convinced that your discomfort is evidence of your character flaws.

Survivors often describe how they learned to dismiss their own discomfort with boundary violations as proof that they were indeed "too sensitive" or "making a big deal out of nothing." The identity attacks provided the justification for accepting treatment that healthy boundaries would have rejected.

Boundary Violations Enable Emotional Parentification

When your boundaries have been consistently violated, you don't develop a clear sense of where you end and others begin. This makes it easier for narcissistic parents to make you responsible for their emotional well-being.

If you haven't learned that your emotions belong to you, it feels normal when you're asked to manage someone else's emotions. If you haven't developed a sense of psychological autonomy, taking responsibility for adult problems feels like what you're supposed to do.

The lack of healthy boundaries makes it difficult to recognize when you're being asked to take on inappropriate emotional responsibilities. Without a clear sense of what's yours and what belongs to others, emotional parentification feels like natural caregiving rather than inappropriate burden-shifting.

Emotional Parentification Reinforces Identity Attacks

When you're forced to be the family's emotional manager, it seems to confirm that your role is to serve others rather than to have your own needs met. This reinforces the identity attacks that tell you you're selfish for wanting care or attention.

The parentification makes the identity attacks feel true. If your value comes from managing other people's emotions, then having your own emotions or needs does feel selfish and inappropriate.

Clinical work reveals how this cycle becomes self-reinforcing: the more you function as the family's emotional manager, the more evidence it seems to provide that this is your proper role, making it increasingly difficult to imagine having your own emotional needs or boundaries.

The Long-Term Developmental Damage

Understanding these three pillars helps explain why the damage from narcissistic parenting feels so fundamental and why healing can be so challenging. These weren't isolated incidents of poor parenting—they were systematic attacks on the basic building blocks of healthy psychological development.

Disrupted Sense of Self

The combination of identity attacks, boundary violations, and emotional parentification prevents children from developing a stable, authentic sense of self. Instead of learning who they are and what they need, they learn to be whoever they need to be to survive.

As an adult, you might struggle with knowing what you want, what you like, or who you are when you're not performing a role for someone else. Your sense of identity might feel fluid, uncertain, or dependent on external validation.

This disrupted sense of self isn't just confusion—it's the natural result of spending your developmental years focused on survival and others' needs rather than on the normal process of self-discovery and identity formation.

Impaired Relationship Skills

These three pillars teach profoundly unhealthy lessons about relationships. You learn that love is conditional on performance, that boundaries are selfish, and that your role is to manage other people's emotions.

As an adult, you might struggle with intimacy, have difficulty maintaining healthy boundaries, or find yourself repeatedly in relationships where you give much more than you receive.

The relationship skills you developed were optimized for surviving in dysfunctional relationships rather than thriving in healthy ones. Learning to relate in healthy ways often requires unlearning these survival-based relationship patterns.

Chronic Self-Doubt

The systematic attacks on your perception, identity, and autonomy create lasting self-doubt that extends far beyond your relationship with your family. You might question your memories, doubt your emotional reactions, or struggle to trust your own judgment about people and situations.

This self-doubt makes you vulnerable to future manipulation and abuse because you've learned not to trust your own warning signals or protective instincts. Survivors often describe how they dismiss red flags in relationships because they've been taught to doubt their own perceptions.

Emotional Dysregulation

The suppression of your emotional development while being forced to manage others' emotions creates lasting difficulties with emotional regulation. You might feel overwhelmed by emotions when they surface, struggle to identify what you're feeling, or find it difficult to tolerate emotional intensity.

Recovery work shows that many survivors swing between emotional numbness and emotional overwhelm because they never learned healthy emotional regulation skills during their crucial developmental years.

The Intergenerational Nature of the Damage

One of the most important things to understand about these three pillars is that they often represent intergenerational patterns of abuse. Clinical observations suggest that your narcissistic parent likely experienced similar treatment in their own childhood, and without conscious intervention and healing, these patterns get passed down through families.

This doesn't excuse the abuse you experienced, but it helps explain why it was so systematic and why it felt so deeply embedded in your family's way of operating. These weren't conscious choices to harm you—they were unconscious repetitions of learned patterns of relating.

Understanding the intergenerational nature of these patterns also highlights the importance of your healing work. By breaking these cycles in your own life, you prevent them from being passed on to future generations.

Breaking the Cycle

The fact that you're reading this book and working to understand these patterns means you're already beginning to break the cycle. Conscious awareness of these dynamics is the first step toward healing and preventing their repetition.

Healing from the three pillars of destruction involves rebuilding an authentic sense of self, learning to establish and maintain healthy boundaries, developing your own emotional regulation skills, and learning to have relationships based on mutual care rather than caretaking.

This healing work is not just for you—it's for every relationship you'll have going forward and potentially for children who might benefit from your increased emotional health and awareness.

In the next chapter, we'll explore how to process the intense emotions that arise when you fully recognize the extent of the damage that was done to you. Understanding these three pillars often brings up righteous anger, profound grief, and sometimes overwhelming rage. Learning to feel and process these emotions safely is a crucial part of your healing journey.

The systematic nature of what was done to you wasn't your fault, and recognizing it isn't about blame or victimhood—it's about understanding so you can heal. These three pillars that were used to break you down can now become the foundation for understanding how to build yourself back up.

7

THE COMPLETE FAMILY CIRCUS

UNDERSTANDING THE CAST OF CHARACTERS IN DYSFUNCTIONAL FAMILY SYSTEMS

I need to tell you something that might be hard to hear: your family wasn't just one toxic person making bad choices. What you lived through was an entire system, a carefully orchestrated performance where everyone had a role to play. I know this because I lived it too, and understanding these roles was one of the most important breakthroughs in my healing journey.

When I first learned about family roles in dysfunctional systems, I felt this mix of relief and rage. Relief because suddenly everything made sense. Rage because I realized how calculated it all was. You weren't dealing with individual family members who happened to treat you badly. You were caught in a machine designed to keep everyone in their assigned positions, and your position was at the bottom.

The Narcissistic Parent: The Puppet Master Behind the Curtain

The Director of Your Suffering

Let me start with the person at the center of it all. The narcissistic parent operates like a theater director, but instead of creating art, they create chaos. They assign roles, control the narrative, and make sure everyone stays in character. I remember watching my narcissistic mother orchestrate family drama like she was conducting a symphony of dysfunction.

Research shows that narcissistic parents cannot tolerate being seen as flawed. Dr. Karyl McBride's work on narcissistic mothers reveals how these parents create elaborate systems to project their inadequacies onto others, particularly onto us, their scapegoats. They need someone to blame for every family problem, and that someone became you.

The Emotional Terrorist

What I've learned is that narcissistic parents rule through emotional terrorism. They create artificial scarcity of love and approval, making everyone compete for scraps of their attention. I used to watch my siblings practically perform circus tricks trying to win a moment of genuine approval that never came.

The narcissistic parent's power doesn't come from strength but from their willingness to destroy anyone who threatens their false image. They keep everyone walking on eggshells, never knowing when the next explosion will come. The whole family learns that peace depends on keeping the narcissist happy, and keeping them happy often means joining them in scapegoating you.

The Golden Child: The Favored Actor in a Rigged Game

The Chosen One Who Pays in Different Currency

The golden child was your narcissistic parent's chosen favorite, the one who could do no wrong. They received the praise, attention, and resources that were denied to you.

But here's what I learned that changed everything: the golden child's position comes at a terrible cost. They must suppress their authentic self to maintain their favored status. In her clinical work with narcissistic families, Dr. Stephanie Donaldson-Pressman observed that golden children often develop their own narcissistic traits or become deeply anxious, knowing their position depends on maintaining impossible perfection.

The Beautiful Prison

The golden child becomes an extension of the narcissistic parent rather than an independent person. They learn to read the parent's moods perfectly, to reflect back exactly what the parent wants to see. Some golden children genuinely believe they are superior to you because they've internalized the family narrative. Others feel guilty but are too afraid to speak up because they know that challenging the system means losing everything.

I had to learn to see my golden child sibling as trapped in their role just like I was trapped in mine, just in a more comfortable prison. This understanding didn't excuse their cruelty, but it helped me stop taking their behavior so personally.

The Enabler: The Supporting Actor Who Enables Your Destruction

The "Nicer" Parent Who Never Saves You

The enabling parent appears to be the "nice one," the reasonable voice in the chaos. They might offer comfort and understanding, but their primary function is maintaining the dysfunctional system by making it bearable enough that nobody leaves.

I remember my enabling father saying things like "That's just how your mother is" or "She doesn't mean it" or "Try to understand, she's under stress." These words felt like comfort in the moment, but I later realized they were teaching me to normalize abuse.

The Betrayal of Inaction

The enabler's role is to normalize the abnormal, to help everyone adjust to dysfunction rather than challenging it. They might rescue you from the worst abuse, but they never address the root cause. Their kindness keeps you hoping that someone in the family truly sees and values you, which makes leaving even harder.

Research on family systems shows that enablers can be victims themselves, too afraid or damaged to fight back. But some are co-conspirators who benefit from the system. Either way, their refusal to protect you when they had the power to do so represents a profound betrayal of their parental duty.

Flying Monkeys: The Recruited Enforcers of Family Lies

The Extended Army of Manipulation

Flying monkeys are family members or friends who carry out the narcissistic parent's wishes, often without fully understanding what they're doing. They spread gossip, relay messages, gather information, and help maintain the family's false narrative about you.

I had flying monkeys who were aunts, grandparents, and family friends. They would contact me with messages like "Your mother is heartbroken" or "Can't you just apologize and make things right?" They positioned themselves as peacemakers while actually serving as agents of manipulation.

The Coordinated Campaign Against Your Reality

Some flying monkeys are true believers who have completely bought into the family mythology. Others are opportunists gaining favor by participating in your persecution. Still others are victims themselves who redirect abuse toward you to avoid becoming targets.

The presence of flying monkeys made me feel crazy and isolated. When multiple people tell you that you're wrong, that your perceptions are false, that you need to change, it becomes incredibly difficult to trust your own reality. I learned this isn't accidental. It's a coordinated campaign to break down your sense of truth.

The Lost Child: The Invisible Survivor

The Ghost in the Family Portrait

The lost child copes with family dysfunction by becoming invisible. They withdraw emotionally and physically, spending time alone in their rooms, losing themselves in books, fantasy, or online worlds. They learn that safety comes from not being noticed.

Sometimes you were both the scapegoat and the lost child, alternately targeted for abuse and then ignored when you withdrew. I remember disappearing into my room for hours, becoming so quiet that family members would forget I was there.

The Price of Invisibility

The lost child often becomes the family's "easy" child, the one who never causes problems. But this comes at the cost of their own development. Research shows that children who cope through withdrawal often struggle with depression, anxiety, and dissociative symptoms as they disconnect from their own feelings and experiences.

The Mascot: The Comedian Hiding Behind Laughter

The Entertainer Who Swallows Their Pain

The mascot tries to defuse family tension through humor, charm, and entertainment. They become the class clown, the one who can always make people laugh, who lightens the mood when things get too heavy.

I knew a mascot sibling who could joke about the most serious family problems, minimizing our pain through comedy. But I learned that the mascot's humor is a defense mechanism, a way to avoid dealing with painful realities.

When Laughter Becomes a Prison

The mascot learns to read the room's emotional temperature and provide exactly the right distraction to prevent explosions. But they often struggle with being taken seriously, with accessing their own authentic emotions. They become so good at performing happiness that they lose touch with their true feelings.

The Caretaker: The Child Who Raised the Adults

The Little Parent Who Lost Their Childhood

The caretaker takes on adult responsibilities, often becoming a parent to their siblings or even to their parents. They cook, clean, provide emotional support, and try to hold the family together through sheer force of will.

As the scapegoat, you might have also been the caretaker, desperately trying to fix the family problems that were being blamed on you. I remember feeling responsible for everyone's emotions, believing that if I could just be good enough, care enough, do enough, I could heal our broken family.

The Burden of Premature Responsibility

The caretaker may seem mature and responsible, earning praise for being "so good with the family." But this premature responsibility robs them of normal childhood development. They learn to meet others' needs while ignoring their own, setting up a lifetime pattern of codependency and self-neglect.

The Fluid Nature of Family Roles

When the Script Changes

These roles aren't permanent or mutually exclusive. I watched family members switch roles depending on circumstances or family crises. A golden child could become a scapegoat if they challenged the parent's authority. You might have played multiple roles throughout your childhood, or different roles with different family members.

The common thread is that none of these roles allowed you to simply be yourself, a child deserving of love and protection regardless of what you provided to the family system.

Understanding the System's True Purpose

The Machine That Required Your Suffering

All of these roles serve the same ultimate purpose: maintaining the narcissistic parent's false image and avoiding accountability for the family's problems. Each role deflects attention from the real source of dysfunction and keeps family members too busy managing their assigned parts to question the system itself.

Your scapegoat role was crucial because it provided an explanation for all family problems that didn't implicate the truly responsible parties. As long as you were available to blame, the narcissistic parent never had to face their failures, the enabling parent never had to take action, and the other family members never had to acknowledge their complicity.

Breaking Free from the Performance

Seeing the Truth Behind the Curtain

Understanding these roles was devastating and liberating for me. Devastating because it revealed the calculated nature of my family's treatment. Liberating because it removed the burden of personal responsibility for my family's dysfunction.

You cannot fix a system that requires your suffering to function. You cannot earn love from people who need you to be unlovable to maintain their own psychological equilibrium.

Your Family Members Were Trapped Too

The roles your family members played don't excuse their behavior, but understanding those roles helped me stop taking their actions personally. The golden child who joined in my persecution was protecting their position. The enabler who failed to defend me was avoiding becoming a target. The flying monkeys who spread lies about me were serving the system that gave their lives structure and meaning.

None of this makes their treatment acceptable. But it helps you understand that their behavior was about the system they were trapped in, not about who you truly are.

Reflection Questions:

How does understanding these family roles change your perspective on your childhood experiences?

Which family members do you now see as trapped in their roles versus actively choosing to harm you?

What would it mean for your healing to stop taking their behavior personally?

How might your relationships with family members change if you saw them as playing assigned roles?

Your Freedom Lies in Leaving the Theater

You Don't Need to Audition for a Better Role

Your healing involves rejecting not just the scapegoat role but the entire family circus. You don't have to audition for a better part in their dysfunctional drama. You can leave the theater entirely and create your own authentic life.

The family circus continues without you, but that's no longer your concern. Your concern now is discovering who you really are when you're not playing a role, when you're not managing others' emotions, when you're not accepting blame for problems you didn't create.

That person, your authentic self, is worth fighting for. They're worth protecting. They're worth loving exactly as they are. And I promise you, as someone who has walked this path, that person is more beautiful and valuable than any role you were ever forced to play.

8

SYSTEMATIC VS. NORMAL

ABUSE VS. CONFLICT

One of the most important distinctions you need to understand in your healing journey is recognizing what you actually experienced. For years, I minimized what happened to me by calling it "a difficult childhood" or "imperfect parenting." I told myself that every family has problems, that my parents did their best with what they had.

While there's some truth in recognizing that hurt people often hurt people, there's also danger in using this understanding to excuse what was actually systematic abuse. What happened to you wasn't just family conflict or poor parenting skills. It was calculated, persistent, and designed to break down your sense of self.

Understanding this distinction isn't about creating a victim mentality or assigning blame. It's about validation, clarity, and helping you understand why traditional approaches to "family healing" haven't worked for you. The tools that help people move past normal family conflict are completely inadequate for healing from systematic abuse.

Normal Conflict vs. Systematic Abuse

When Families Fight but Love Remains

Healthy families have conflict. Parents get overwhelmed, siblings fight, mistakes are made, and feelings get hurt. I've watched healthy families navigate disagreements, and what struck me wasn't the absence of problems but how those problems were handled.

In healthy families, conflict happens within a foundation of love, respect, and genuine care for each family member's wellbeing. Parents may lose their temper, but they apologize when they're wrong. Siblings may fight, but there's no systematic campaign to destroy one child's sense of worth. Most importantly, mistakes are acknowledged and repair is possible.

Research on healthy family dynamics shows several key characteristics that distinguish normal conflict from abuse. There's proportionality between the issue and the response. If a child breaks a rule, the consequence fits the infraction. If a parent overreacts, they recognize it and make amends.

The Systematic Nature of Family Abuse

Systematic abuse is entirely different in both its nature and its purpose. While healthy families use conflict to solve problems and maintain relationships, abusive families use conflict to maintain power, control, and psychological dominance over the designated target.

The word "systematic" is crucial here. This isn't random cruelty or isolated incidents of poor parenting. It's a coordinated approach to maintaining family dysfunction through the destruction of one member's psychological development.

I remember the moment I realized that what happened to me wasn't a series of unfortunate parenting mistakes but a systematic pattern designed to keep me psychologically subordinated to the family system. The scapegoat's suffering serves specific functions: it provides an explanation for family problems that doesn't implicate the truly responsible parties, and it maintains the narcissistic parent's false image by projecting all negativity onto the designated target.

The Presence of Gaslighting

Perhaps the most telling difference between normal conflict and systematic abuse is the presence of gaslighting. In healthy families, when someone is hurt, their pain is acknowledged even if the intention wasn't to cause harm. The focus is on understanding what happened and preventing future harm.

In systematically abusive families, the victim's perception of reality is consistently undermined. "That never happened." "You're remembering it wrong." "You're being too sensitive." These responses aren't attempts to understand different perspectives; they're attempts to maintain control by making you doubt your own perceptions and sanity.

Ways Narcissistic Parents Destroy Children

Identity Attacks: Destroying Your Sense of Self

The first method of systematic destruction involves attacking your fundamental sense of who you are. This goes far beyond correcting behavior to attacking your core identity. Instead of saying "Please clean your room," narcissistic parents say "You're so lazy." Instead of "That behavior isn't acceptable," they say "You're impossible to deal with."

These character attacks serve multiple purposes. They deflect attention from the parent's own behavior by making you the problem. They prevent you from developing a stable, positive sense of self. Most importantly, they make you question your own perceptions and reality.

I remember being told I was "too sensitive" whenever I had a normal emotional reaction to unfair treatment. Over time, I learned to distrust my own emotional responses and rely on others to tell me what was real. This systematic undermining of your sense of self creates lasting self-doubt that extends far beyond your relationship with your family.

Boundary Violations: Teaching You That You Don't Own Yourself

The second pillar involves systematic violations of your physical, emotional, and psychological boundaries. Your body wasn't treated as your own. Your emotions were not treated as valid. Your thoughts and inner world were not respected as separate from your parent's.

Physical boundaries teach children that they have a right to bodily autonomy and personal space. When these boundaries are consistently violated through forced affection, room searches, or destruction of personal belongings, children learn that their physical selves are not under their own control.

Emotional boundaries were violated when you were told how you should feel, when your authentic emotions were dismissed as wrong, or when you were made responsible for managing your parent's emotional state. You learned that your emotions existed to serve others rather than to provide information about your own needs and experiences.

Emotional Parentification: Stealing Your Childhood

The third method involves forcing you to take on adult emotional responsibilities while your own emotional development was ignored or actively suppressed. You became the family's emotional manager, expected to provide support during crises, mediate conflicts, or serve as a confidant for adult problems.

This role reversal is profoundly damaging because it prevents children from developing their own emotional regulation skills while burdening them with responsibilities they're not equipped to handle. You learned that your value came from your ability to manage other people's emotions and solve their problems.

The psychological burden of being responsible for adult emotions while still being a child creates lasting confusion about appropriate relationship dynamics and personal responsibility. As an adult, you might struggle with accepting help, feel uncomfortable with vulnerability, or automatically assume responsibility for managing other people's problems.

When Discipline Becomes Destruction

Healthy discipline is about teaching children appropriate behavior and helping them develop internal regulation skills. It's corrective, proportional, and focused on helping the child learn and grow. The goal is to guide the child toward better choices while maintaining their sense of worth and dignity.

What you experienced wasn't discipline; it was punishment designed to break your spirit and maintain control. The goal wasn't to teach you anything constructive but to ensure your psychological submission to the family hierarchy.

I learned to recognize the difference by examining the intent and the outcome. Healthy discipline helps children feel secure in their parents' love while learning to make better choices. What I experienced made me feel fundamentally flawed and unworthy of love, with no clear path to earning approval or safety.

The Escalation Pattern

In dysfunctional families, punishment often escalates far beyond what any reasonable person would consider appropriate for the "offense." A minor mistake becomes evidence of your fundamental character flaws. A normal childhood behavior becomes proof that you're selfish, lazy, or defiant.

This escalation serves to keep you off-balance and hypervigilant. You never know when the next explosion will come or what might trigger it. The unpredictability is part of the control mechanism, ensuring that you remain focused on avoiding punishment rather than on normal childhood development.

The Absence of Teaching

Real discipline includes teaching. Parents explain why certain behaviors are problematic, help children understand the impact of their actions, and provide guidance for making better choices in the future. The child learns not just what not to do but what to do instead.

Systematic punishment offers no such teaching. You were expected to figure out the ever-changing rules through trial and error, with each error resulting in emotional devastation. The focus was on your inadequacy rather than on learning and growth.

Healthy Families vs. Narcissistic Systems

The Foundation of Unconditional Love

The most fundamental difference between healthy families and narcissistic systems is the presence or absence of unconditional love. In healthy families, love isn't earned through performance; it's given freely because of your inherent worth as a family member.

Children in healthy families know that while their behavior might be corrected, their place in the family is secure. They can make mistakes, have bad days, disagree with their parents, and express their authentic emotions without fear of emotional abandonment or systematic punishment.

In narcissistic family systems, love is conditional on meeting the narcissistic parent's needs and maintaining the dysfunctional status quo. Your worth fluctuates based on how well you perform your assigned role and how effectively you serve the system's needs.

Individual Growth vs. System Maintenance

Healthy families prioritize the individual growth and development of each family member. Parents may have their own needs and limitations, but the overall family structure supports each person's journey toward becoming their authentic self.

Narcissistic family systems prioritize maintaining the system itself, even at the expense of individual family members' wellbeing. Your authentic self was seen as a threat to be managed rather than a treasure to be nurtured. Personal growth was discouraged if it challenged the family's dysfunction or threatened the narcissistic parent's control.

Repair and Accountability

In healthy families, when harm occurs, there's genuine accountability and repair. Parents acknowledge their mistakes, apologize sincerely, and work to do better. Family members can express hurt feelings and be heard. Conflict becomes an opportunity for growth and deeper understanding.

In narcissistic systems, accountability flows only upward. You're held accountable for everyone's emotions and problems, but the narcissistic parent never takes responsibility for their harmful behavior. Attempts to address legitimate grievances are met with defensiveness, blame-shifting, or punishment.

Preparing Children for Life

The ultimate goal of healthy parenting is to prepare children to become independent, emotionally regulated adults capable of forming healthy relationships. Parents gradually increase children's autonomy and responsibility while providing guidance and support.

Narcissistic family systems create either overly dependent children who can't function without the system's approval or hyper-independent children who struggle to trust others or accept help. Neither extreme serves the child's actual development needs.

Why This Recognition Matters

Understanding that you experienced systematic abuse rather than normal family conflict has real implications for your healing journey. The approaches that help people move past normal family difficulties often retraumatize survivors of systematic abuse.

Well-meaning therapists might encourage you to "see your parents' perspective" or "practice forgiveness" without understanding that these approaches can be harmful when applied to systematic abuse situations. You need trauma-informed approaches that prioritize your safety and validate your reality.

Permission to Protect Yourself

Recognizing the systematic nature of what you experienced gives you permission to protect yourself in ways that might seem "extreme" to others. Going no contact, refusing family events, or declining to provide explanations for your boundaries might seem harsh for normal family conflict, but they're often necessary for healing from systematic abuse.

You don't owe abusive family members the same consideration you would give to family members who genuinely made mistakes within a foundation of love. Your healing doesn't require you to minimize what happened or take responsibility for repair with people who systematically destroyed your sense of self.

The clarity that comes from understanding this distinction is both devastating and liberating. Devastating because it confirms the calculated nature of what was done to you. Liberating because it removes the burden of trying to fix something that was designed to be broken.

In our next chapter, we'll explore the anger that naturally arises when you fully recognize how your boundaries were violated and your development was sabotaged. This anger isn't a character flaw; it's a healthy response to genuine injustice, and learning to feel it safely is crucial for your healing.

Part III: Processing It All

9

YOUR RAGE IS JUSTIFIED

ANGER & IMPACT

I need to tell you something that might surprise you: your anger is not only justified, it's necessary. For years, you may have been told that your anger is too much, too intense, or evidence that you haven't "moved on" or "forgiven." You may have been made to feel ashamed of your rage, as if feeling angry about systematic abuse makes you somehow broken or stuck.

Let me be clear: your anger is appropriate. It's proportional. It's healthy. And it's one of the most important emotions you can access on your healing journey.

When I first allowed myself to feel the full force of my rage about what was done to me, it was terrifying. I had spent so many years suppressing it, minimizing it, turning it inward against myself. I was afraid that if I let myself really feel it, I would be consumed by it, that I would become someone I didn't want to be.

What I discovered instead was that my anger was trying to protect me. It was information about boundaries that had been crossed. It was my psyche's way of saying, "What happened to you was wrong, and you deserved better." Learning to feel and honor this anger was crucial to my healing.

The Righteous Anger: Your Boundaries Were Crossed

Your Anger Has a Purpose

Anger is not a character flaw or a sign of weakness. It's a protective emotion designed to alert you when your boundaries have been violated, when you're being treated unfairly, when your safety or wellbeing is threatened. In healthy situations, anger motivates appropriate action to protect yourself and restore justice.

Your anger about what happened to you is what psychologists call "righteous anger." This isn't rage born from entitlement or self-ishness. It's the natural response of a healthy psyche to genuine injustice. Your boundaries weren't just crossed; they were systematically demolished by people who were supposed to protect them.

Research on trauma recovery consistently shows that accessing appropriate anger is a crucial stage in healing from abuse. Dr. Judith Herman's groundbreaking work on trauma recovery identifies the importance of moving from numbness and self-blame to healthy anger as part of the recovery process.

The Scope of What Was Taken From You

Sometimes we minimize our anger because we think what happened wasn't "that bad" compared to others. But consider the scope of what was systematically taken from you. You were robbed of a childhood where you could simply be a child. You were denied the experience of unconditional love and acceptance. Your sense of reality was undermined, your emotions were invalidated, and your developing sense of self was under constant attack.

You were forced to develop survival skills that no child should need. You learned to monitor adult emotions, to manage family dysfunction, to suppress your own needs and feelings. You were made responsible for problems you didn't create and blamed for conflicts you had no power to resolve.

The people who were supposed to nurture and protect you instead used their power to harm you. They took advantage of your natural dependence and trust to serve their own psychological needs. This wasn't just unfortunate or imperfect parenting; it was a profound betrayal of the most fundamental human relationship.

The Compound Interest of Betrayal

What makes this betrayal even more devastating is that it happened during your most vulnerable developmental years. The damage wasn't just what they did to you in those moments; it was how that treatment shaped your entire understanding of yourself, relationships, and the world.

Your anger isn't just about past events. It's about how those events continue to impact your life today. It's about the relationships you've struggled to build, the self-doubt that follows you, the hypervigilance that exhausts you, the emotional regulation challenges you face as an adult.

You're not just angry about what they did; you're angry about what they stole from you. The confidence you might have had, the trust that could have been your foundation, the sense of inherent worth that should have been your birthright. Your anger encompasses not just what was, but what could have been.

Permission to Feel Your Anger

One of the biggest fears many survivors have about their anger is that feeling it makes them like their abusers. This fear often keeps people trapped in emotional numbness or self-directed rage. Let me be clear: feeling angry about abuse does not make you abusive.

Your narcissistic family members used anger as a weapon to control and intimidate. They expressed rage to maintain power and avoid accountability. Their anger was often disproportionate, unpredictable, and designed to harm others.

Your anger is fundamentally different. It's a response to genuine injustice. It's proportional to the harm that was done. It's not about controlling others but about honoring your own worth and protecting your boundaries. Learning to distinguish between healthy anger and abusive rage is part of your healing process.

You Don't Have to Forgive to Heal

Many survivors feel pressure to forgive their abusers as a condition of healing. This pressure often comes from well-meaning people who don't understand the nature of systematic abuse, or from religious or cultural messages that equate forgiveness with virtue.

Forgiveness is a personal choice that can only come from you, if and when you're ready. It cannot be forced, rushed, or imposed from the outside. Some survivors find forgiveness helpful in their healing journey; others find it retraumatizing or inappropriate for their situation.

What's crucial for healing is not forgiveness but truth-telling, validation, and the restoration of your sense of worth and agency. You can heal completely without ever forgiving your abusers. Your healing is not dependent on your ability to minimize their actions or find compassion for their circumstances.

Anger as Self-Advocacy

Learning to feel your anger appropriately is actually a form of self-advocacy. When you honor your anger about what was done to you, you're saying that your wellbeing matters, that you deserved better treatment, that what happened was not acceptable.

This is revolutionary for many survivors who have spent years minimizing their experiences or taking responsibility for their abuse. Anger interrupts the pattern of self-blame and self-attack. It redirects your emotional energy toward the appropriate targets: the people who chose to harm you.

I remember the first time I allowed myself to feel truly angry at my mother instead of angry at myself for not being "good enough" to earn her love. It was a profound shift. Instead of feeling defective, I felt wronged. Instead of feeling hopeless, I felt empowered. My anger was telling me that I had value and that her treatment of me was unacceptable.

Anger as Information and Protection

Anger carries important information about your values, boundaries, and needs. When you feel angry about your past treatment, you're identifying what matters to you, what you consider unacceptable, what kind of treatment you deserve.

This information is crucial for building healthy relationships and making decisions that honor your wellbeing. Your anger about being dismissed and invalidated tells you that you value being heard and understood. Your anger about having your boundaries violated tells you that respect for your autonomy is non-negotiable.

Learning to listen to your anger helps you identify red flags in current relationships. If someone's behavior triggers the same anger you feel about your family's treatment, that's important information about whether this person is safe for you.

Anger as Boundary Enforcement

Healthy anger motivates boundary setting and enforcement. When someone treats you in ways that trigger your righteous anger, that emotion can fuel your ability to speak up, set limits, or remove yourself from harmful situations.

Many survivors struggle with boundary setting because they've been conditioned to prioritize others' comfort over their own wellbeing. Accessing your anger about past boundary violations can provide the emotional energy needed to protect your boundaries in the present.

Your anger says, "This is not acceptable," and provides the internal support needed to act on that awareness. Without access to appropriate anger, you might continue to accept treatment that feels familiar but harmful.

The Protective Function of Rage

Sometimes anger escalates to rage, and this can feel frightening or overwhelming. But even rage serves a protective function. Rage is anger's emergency response, activated when threats feel extreme or when other protective responses have failed.

If you experience rage when thinking about your family's treatment, this isn't evidence that you're out of control or becoming like them. It's evidence that your psyche recognizes the severity of what was done to you and is mobilizing all available resources to protect you.

Rage can provide the emotional fuel needed to make difficult but necessary changes: leaving toxic relationships, going no contact with abusive family members, or standing up to people who try to minimize your experience.

Processing Rage Safely

Creating Safe Containers for Your Anger

While your anger is justified and necessary, it's important to find safe ways to feel and express it. Anger that's been suppressed for years can feel overwhelming when it finally surfaces. Having strategies for processing it safely protects both you and your relationships.

Physical exercise can be an excellent outlet for angry energy. Running, boxing, martial arts, or even vigorous dancing can help you move the energy through your body. Some people find relief in screaming into pillows, hitting punching bags, or engaging in other physical expressions of anger in private spaces.

Writing can also be a powerful tool for processing anger. Uncensored journaling, writing letters you never send, or creating detailed accounts of your anger can help you understand and release it. The goal isn't to create literary masterpieces but to give your anger a voice.

Therapeutic Support for Anger Work

Working with a trauma-informed therapist can provide crucial support for processing anger safely. Many survivors have never learned how to feel and express anger appropriately because it was either forbidden or modeled destructively in their families.

A skilled therapist can help you distinguish between different types of anger, learn healthy expression techniques, and work through the fear and shame that often surround this emotion. They can also help you understand how your anger connects to your healing and how to use it constructively.

Some therapeutic approaches, like EMDR or somatic therapies, can be particularly helpful for processing anger that's stored in the body. These approaches recognize that anger isn't just a mental or emotional experience but a whole-body phenomenon that needs to be addressed holistically.

Anger Without Action

It's important to understand that feeling anger doesn't obligate you to take immediate action. You can be furious with your family members without confronting them. You can rage about what was done to you without needing to express that rage directly to the people who harmed you.

Sometimes the safest and most healing choice is to feel your anger fully in therapeutic or private settings without engaging with the people who triggered it. This is particularly important when dealing with people who are likely to use your anger against you or who might escalate conflicts in dangerous ways.

Your anger is yours to feel and process. How you choose to express it or act on it depends on your circumstances, safety considerations, and personal values. The healing comes from honoring the emotion itself, not from any particular expression of it.

Integration and Wisdom

As you learn to process your anger safely, it gradually transforms from overwhelming rage into integrated wisdom. You develop the ability to feel anger without being consumed by it, to use its information without being controlled by it.

This integrated anger becomes a reliable internal compass, alerting you to boundary violations and motivating appropriate self-protection. It no longer feels like a dangerous emotion to be suppressed but like a valuable ally in your healing and self-advocacy.

You learn to trust your anger's messages while maintaining agency over your responses. This is emotional maturity: not the absence of anger, but the ability to feel it, understand it, and choose how to respond to it in ways that serve your wellbeing.

The Transformation of Anger

Accessing and processing your righteous anger is part of the transformation from victim to survivor. Victims feel helpless and blame themselves. Survivors feel angry about injustice and take action to protect themselves.

This doesn't mean survivors are constantly angry or that anger defines them. It means they have access to the full range of their emotions, including the protective ones that help them recognize and respond to threats to their wellbeing.

Your anger is evidence that you know you deserved better. It's proof that despite years of conditioning to accept unacceptable treatment, some part of you maintained awareness of your worth and value. Honoring this anger is honoring the part of you that refused to be completely broken.

Anger as Fuel for Change

Many survivors find that their anger, once processed and integrated, becomes fuel for positive change. They use their understanding of injustice to help others, to create safer environments, to break cycles of abuse in their own families.

This doesn't mean you're obligated to become an advocate or helper. But many people find that their processed anger gives them clarity about what matters to them and energy to create change in whatever sphere feels meaningful to them.

Your anger about what was done to you can become passion for what you want to create instead. The rage about being silenced can become commitment to having a voice. The fury about being ignored can become determination to be seen and valued.

In our next chapter, we'll explore the complex family dynamics that worked together to create and maintain your scapegoat role. Understanding these dynamics helps explain why individual family members behaved as they did and why the system was so resistant to change. This knowledge can help you stop taking their behavior personally and focus your energy on your own healing rather than on trying to fix irreparable family relationships.

10

THE FAMILY CONSPIRACY

DYNAMICS & TRIANGULATION

What you experienced wasn't just one person's cruelty or poor parenting choices. What happened to you was a conspiracy, a coordinated effort by multiple family members to maintain a dysfunctional system that required your suffering to function. Understanding this conspiracy is crucial because it helps you stop personalizing their behavior and start seeing it as the systematic manipulation it was.

I used to think that if I could just figure out the right words, the right approach, the right way to be, I could make my family see me and treat me fairly. I spent decades trying to earn what should have been given freely: basic respect, consideration, and love. What I didn't understand was that their treatment of me wasn't based on who I was or what I did. It was based on who they needed me to be for their system to work.

The family conspiracy against the scapegoat involves specific roles, tactics, and dynamics that work together to maintain the status quo. Once you understand how these elements function, you can stop wasting energy trying to change people who benefit from your pain and focus that energy on healing and protecting yourself.

The Golden Child vs. Scapegoat Dynamic

The Manufactured Competition

The relationship between the golden child and the scapegoat isn't natural sibling rivalry. It's a manufactured competition created and maintained by the narcissistic parent to serve their own psychological needs. This dynamic ensures that the children never unite against the real source of family dysfunction.

In healthy families, parents work to minimize competition between siblings and help them develop supportive relationships with each other. They celebrate each child's unique strengths without creating comparisons that make one child feel superior and another feel inadequate.

In narcissistic family systems, the parent actively cultivates competition, comparison, and resentment between siblings. They praise one child for the same behavior they punish in another. They share private information about one child with others, breaking confidentiality and trust. They create artificial scarcity where children must compete for attention, approval, and resources.

The Psychological Purpose of the Split

This split serves several important functions for the narcissistic parent. First, it provides them with a clear "good" child who reflects positively on their parenting and a "bad" child who can be blamed for all family problems. This arrangement protects their self-image while giving them someone to scapegoat.

Second, the competition between siblings prevents them from forming alliances that might challenge the parent's authority. As long as the golden child feels superior to the scapegoat and the scapegoat feels inferior to the golden child, neither child questions the system that created this hierarchy.

I remember watching my golden child sibling enjoy privileges I was denied, knowing that pointing this out would only result in more punishment for me and more praise for them. The system was designed to make me feel crazy for noticing the unfairness while simultaneously making that unfairness impossible to ignore.

The Golden Child's Investment in Your Pain

Understanding the golden child's psychology is crucial for your healing because it helps explain why they often actively participate in your scapegoating rather than defending you. The golden child's privileged position depends on your subordinated position. If you were treated fairly, their special status would disappear.

This creates a psychological investment in maintaining your scapegoat role. The golden child learns that keeping you "in your place" protects their position in the family hierarchy. They may participate in your persecution not out of sadistic pleasure but out of fear of losing their favored status.

Research on family systems shows that golden children often struggle with anxiety about maintaining their position. They learn to read the narcissistic parent's moods carefully and adjust their behavior to maintain approval. Defending you or questioning your treatment threatens their security, so they choose their own survival over fairness or sibling loyalty.

The Trauma Bond That Isn't

Many scapegoats hope that shared trauma will eventually create a bond with their golden child sibling. They imagine that as adults, their sibling will recognize the dysfunction and they can heal together. This hope often leads to repeated disappointment and retraumatization.

The truth is that the golden child and scapegoat had fundamentally different childhood experiences. While both were harmed by the dysfunctional system, their adaptations and coping mechanisms developed in opposite directions. The golden child learned to maintain position through compliance and superiority. The scapegoat learned to survive through hypervigilance and self-protection.

These different survival strategies often make adult relationships between former golden children and scapegoats very difficult. The golden child may continue to need to feel superior, while the scapegoat seeks equality and validation. The golden child may minimize family dysfunction to protect their memories, while the scapegoat needs acknowledgment of the abuse they endured.

Triangulation, Flying Monkeys & Family Games

Triangulation is one of the most insidious tactics used in dysfunctional families. Instead of addressing conflicts directly, family members communicate through third parties, spreading information, creating alliances, and manipulating relationships to maintain control and avoid accountability.

In healthy families, people communicate directly with each other about problems and work toward resolution. If Parent A has an issue with Child B, they speak to Child B directly. If siblings have a conflict, parents help them work it out rather than taking sides or spreading gossip about the situation.

In narcissistic family systems, the narcissistic parent becomes the central hub of all communication, controlling the flow of information and manipulating family members' perceptions of each other. They might tell you that your sibling said something hurtful about you, then tell your sibling that you're angry at them, creating conflict where none existed.

The Flying Monkey Network

Flying monkeys extend the narcissistic parent's reach far beyond what they could accomplish alone. These are family members, friends, or extended family who carry out the narcissist's wishes, often without fully understanding their role in the manipulation.

Some flying monkeys are true believers who have completely bought into the family mythology about you. They genuinely believe you're the problem and see themselves as helping by encouraging you to "be reasonable" or "make peace with your family."

Others are opportunists who gain favor by participating in your persecution.

Still others are fellow victims who redirect abuse toward you to avoid becoming targets themselves. They may feel guilty about their participation but are too afraid of the consequences to stand up for you or challenge the system.

The Information War

Controlling information is crucial to maintaining the conspiracy against you. The narcissistic family system operates on carefully managed narratives about each family member, and these narratives must be protected from contradictory evidence.

Your perspective threatens these narratives because it reveals the truth about family dynamics. This is why your attempts to share your experience are met with such fierce resistance. It's not just that they disagree with your perspective; it's that your perspective threatens the entire foundation of their psychological equilibrium.

The family conspiracy includes coordinated efforts to discredit your version of events, to gaslight you about your memories, and to present alternative explanations for your experiences that protect the family's preferred narrative. They might acknowledge that you were treated differently but claim it was because you were "difficult" or "needed more structure."

The Loyalty Tests

Dysfunctional families often operate through a series of unspoken loyalty tests. Family members prove their allegiance by participating in the scapegoating of the designated target. Refusing to participate or, worse, defending the scapegoat, is seen as betrayal that results in punishment or exclusion.

These loyalty tests explain why family members who privately acknowledge the unfairness of your treatment still participate in it publicly. They know that challenging the system means risking their own position in the family hierarchy. For many people, the fear of becoming the scapegoat themselves is stronger than their moral objections to what's being done to you.

This dynamic creates a family culture where everyone is complicit in maintaining dysfunction because everyone fears becoming the next target. It's a system based on fear rather than love, control rather than support.

The Enabler's Role in Your Suffering

The Myth of the Innocent Bystander

The enabling parent often presents themselves as the "innocent bystander" who has no power to change the situation. They position themselves as fellow victims of the narcissistic parent's behavior, claiming they're doing their best to survive in a difficult situation.

This narrative is both psychologically convenient and fundamentally dishonest. While the enabling parent may indeed be a victim of the narcissistic parent's abuse, they are also an adult with choices. Their decision to enable rather than protect represents a profound failure of their parental duty.

The enabler's role in the conspiracy is crucial because they provide the narcissistic parent with credibility and cover. Their participation makes the abuse seem normal and acceptable. They serve as witnesses who can confirm that the narcissistic parent isn't "that bad" and that you're "too sensitive" or "remembering things wrong."

The Active Nature of Enabling

Enabling isn't passive; it's an active choice that requires ongoing effort and conscious decision-making. The enabling parent must consistently choose the narcissistic parent's comfort over their child's wellbeing. They must ignore obvious signs of abuse and distress. They must participate in gaslighting and reality distortion.

I used to think my enabling father was just weak or afraid. What I came to understand was that his enabling required constant active choices. He had to choose to ignore my tears, to dismiss my complaints, to excuse her behavior, to blame me for "provoking" her. These weren't unconscious responses; they were deliberate decisions to maintain his position at my expense.

The enabling parent often develops sophisticated strategies for managing the family dysfunction without addressing its root cause. They become expert at damage control, crisis management, and emotional cleanup. Their entire identity becomes organized around managing the narcissistic parent's behavior and its consequences.

The Secondary Gains of Enabling

Enabling provides the secondary parent with certain benefits that help explain their commitment to maintaining the dysfunctional system. They avoid becoming the narcissistic parent's primary target by redirecting that anger toward you. They maintain their position as the "good" parent without having to do the hard work of actually protecting their children.

The enabling parent also benefits from the power structure that puts them above the children in the family hierarchy. Challenging the narcissistic parent's authority might threaten their own adult privileges and require them to take on more responsibility for family problems.

Some enabling parents enjoy feeling needed and important as the family's emotional manager and crisis resolver. Their identity becomes so intertwined with this role that change feels threatening to their sense of self and purpose.

The Enabler's Investment in Your Silence

The enabling parent has a significant investment in your silence about family dysfunction. Your speaking truth threatens their carefully constructed narrative about the family and their role in it. If you're believed, their failure to protect you becomes visible not just to you but to others.

This is why enabling parents often react so strongly to their adult children's attempts to address childhood abuse. They experience your truth-telling as an attack on their character and reputation. They may become defensive, dismissive, or even hostile when confronted with the reality of their failure to protect you.

The enabler's need for you to minimize or deny what happened can be just as intense as the narcissistic parent's need for this denial. They may pressure you to "forgive and forget," to "focus on the positive," or to "understand your mother/father's perspective." All of these responses serve to protect them from accountability for their enabling.

Why You Can't Earn Their Respect

The Systematic Nature of Disrespect

The disrespect you experienced wasn't based on your behavior, character, or worthiness. It was based on your assigned role in the family system. Understanding this is crucial because it helps you stop trying to earn something that was never available to you regardless of your efforts.

In healthy families, respect is given based on each person's inherent human dignity. Children don't have to earn their parents' respect through performance; they receive it because they matter as individuals. When children make mistakes or behave inappropriately, the correction addresses the behavior while preserving respect for the person.

In narcissistic family systems, respect is conditional and hierarchical. The narcissistic parent commands respect but gives none. The golden child receives respect as long as they maintain their position. The scapegoat is systematically denied respect regardless of their behavior because disrespecting them is essential to maintaining the family's power structure.

The Function of Your Devaluation

Your devaluation served specific psychological functions for other family members. It made them feel superior by comparison. It provided a target for displaced anger and frustration. It confirmed their chosen position in the family hierarchy. Most importantly, it absolved them of responsibility for their own problems and limitations.

This systematic devaluation required ongoing maintenance. Every achievement you accomplished had to be minimized or ignored to preserve the narrative of your inadequacy. Every positive quality you displayed had to be reframed as somehow problematic or selfish. Every success you experienced had to be attributed to luck rather than your abilities.

I remember the mental gymnastics my family performed to maintain their negative view of me even when I succeeded. Academic achievements were dismissed as "showing off." Professional success was attributed to "good luck" or "having help." Acts of kindness were reframed as "manipulation" or "trying to look good." No evidence could penetrate their need to see me as fundamentally flawed.

The Impossibility of Change Through Performance

Many scapegoats spend years trying to earn respect through perfect performance. They become overachievers, people-pleasers, and caretakers, hoping that if they can just be good enough, helpful enough, successful enough, their families will finally see their worth.

This strategy is doomed to failure because their disrespect isn't based on your inadequacy; it's based on their need to have someone to disrespect. If you stopped being available for this role, they would either need to find another scapegoat or face their own problems and limitations.

The family system has a vested interest in maintaining your scapegoat status regardless of your behavior. Evidence of your worth threatens their psychological equilibrium. Your success challenges their narrative about family dynamics. Your healing and growth expose their dysfunction.

The Protection of Unchanging Roles

Narcissistic family systems resist change because change threatens everyone's psychological defenses. The narcissistic parent needs someone to blame. The golden child needs someone to feel superior to. The enabler needs someone to focus on instead of addressing their own problems. Flying monkeys need the drama and intrigue that comes from having a family scapegoat.

Your attempts to change the dynamic threaten all of these psychological needs. This is why families often escalate their dysfunction when the scapegoat begins to heal and set boundaries. Your growth exposes the toxicity of their system and challenges everyone's comfortable roles.

The conspiracy against you isn't just about maintaining their comfort; it's about protecting their psychological survival strategies. For many family members, acknowledging your worth would require facing painful truths about themselves and their choices that they're not prepared to handle.

Breaking Free from the Conspiracy

Recognizing the Coordinated Nature

Understanding that what you experienced was a conspiracy rather than individual failures helps you stop taking it personally. Their behavior wasn't about who you were; it was about who they needed you to be for their system to function.

This recognition can be both liberating and heartbreaking. Liberating because it removes the burden of trying to fix relationships that were designed to harm you. Heartbreaking because it confirms that the people who were supposed to love you unconditionally instead participated in a coordinated effort to undermine your sense of worth.

Your Healing Threatens Their System

As you heal and develop healthy boundaries, your family may escalate their efforts to pull you back into your scapegoat role. They may love-bomb you with temporary kindness, guilt you about abandoning the family, or recruit new flying monkeys to pressure you into returning to the dysfunction.

These escalations aren't evidence that you're doing something wrong; they're evidence that you're doing something right. Your healing threatens their psychological equilibrium and forces them to face their own problems without having you to blame.

Freedom Lies in Acceptance

Your freedom lies not in changing their behavior but in accepting its true nature and protecting yourself accordingly. You cannot love them into treating you well. You cannot achieve enough to earn their respect. You cannot heal them through your own suffering.

What you can do is recognize the conspiracy for what it was, validate your own experience, and build a life that reflects your true worth rather than their distorted perceptions. In our next chapter, we'll explore what happens when the family conspiracy escalates to complete ostracization and how to survive the profound emotional abandonment that often follows a scapegoat's attempt to break free from their assigned role.

11

WHEN LOVE BECOMES HATE

THE PAIN OF FAMILY OSTRACIZATION

There comes a moment in many scapegoats' lives when the family's treatment shifts from abuse disguised as love to open hostility and rejection. This transition can be jarring and devastating, but it's also clarifying. When the mask of "family love" finally falls away, you're forced to see the relationship for what it truly was.

I experienced this shift when I began setting boundaries and refusing to accept blame for family problems. What had been framed as "tough love" or "holding me accountable" suddenly became clear hatred and rejection. The family that had claimed to love me despite my "flaws" revealed that their love was entirely conditional on my willingness to serve as their scapegoat.

This transformation from conditional love to outright ostracization is one of the most painful experiences a scapegoat can endure. Yet it's often necessary for healing because it forces you to face the truth about these relationships and make choices about your own wellbeing that you might otherwise avoid.

Ostracization: When Love Becomes Hate

The Unveiling of True Feelings

The shift from abuse disguised as love to open rejection often happens when you begin to heal, set boundaries, or refuse to accept your assigned role. Suddenly, the family members who claimed to care about you reveal feelings that were always there but hidden beneath a veneer of familial obligation.

This unveiling can be shocking because it contradicts everything you were taught about family loyalty and unconditional love. You discover that their "love" was entirely dependent on your willingness to accept mistreatment and serve their psychological needs.

The transition often begins subtly. Invitations stop coming. Phone calls become less frequent. When you do interact, the warmth that existed during your compliant phases is noticeably absent. The family's energy toward you shifts from frustrated disappointment to cold indifference or active hostility.

The Punishment for Growth

What triggers this shift isn't your failure to improve but your success in healing. As you develop healthier boundaries, refuse to accept blame for problems you didn't create, and start prioritizing your own wellbeing, you become less useful to the family system.

The family that once complained about your "problems" now punishes you for solving them. The people who claimed they wanted you to get better reveal that they actually needed you to stay broken. Your healing threatens their psychological equilibrium and forces them to face their own issues without having you to blame.

I remember the confusion I felt when my family's treatment of me worsened as I got healthier. I had expected that therapy, boundary setting, and emotional growth would improve our relationships. Instead, these positive changes seemed to enrage them and accelerate their rejection of me.

The False Choice

During this transition, families often present their scapegoats with a false choice: return to your old role or be completely rejected. They frame this as a reasonable request for you to "be part of the family" or "stop causing problems." In reality, they're demanding that you sacrifice your healing to maintain their dysfunction.

This false choice is designed to make you feel responsible for the family's dissolution. They want you to believe that your refusal to accept abuse is what's breaking up the family, rather than acknowledging that their need to abuse you is the real problem.

The family may escalate their emotional manipulation during this phase, alternating between threats of abandonment and promises of acceptance if you'll just "go back to normal." These tactics are designed to break down your boundaries and pull you back into the dysfunction before you become too strong to manipulate.

The Family's Rejection Campaign

Coordinated Exclusion

When a family decides to ostracize the scapegoat, it often becomes a coordinated campaign involving multiple family members. This isn't a spontaneous reaction but a systematic effort to punish you for refusing to play your assigned role and to send a message to other family members about the consequences of challenging the system.

The rejection campaign typically includes exclusion from family events, holidays, and important milestones. Suddenly, gatherings that you were once expected to attend happen without you. Photos are taken and shared that pointedly exclude you. Family news and updates stop flowing in your direction.

Extended family members who once maintained relationships with you may suddenly become distant or hostile. This often happens because they've been fed a narrative about your "problems" or "difficult behavior" that justifies your exclusion and their participation in it.

The Rewriting of History

Part of the rejection campaign involves rewriting family history to support the narrative that you were always the problem and that your exclusion is justified. Family members selectively remember incidents that support their version of events while conveniently forgetting evidence that contradicts it.

Your childhood achievements are forgotten or minimized. Your acts of kindness and support for family members are erased from the family narrative. Your legitimate grievances about mistreatment are reframed as evidence of your "victim mentality" or "inability to let go of the past."

This historical revision serves multiple purposes. It helps family members feel justified in their rejection of you. It protects them from having to acknowledge their own harmful behavior. Most importantly, it maintains the family mythology that they are good people dealing with a difficult family member rather than participants in a system of abuse.

The Smear Campaign

Many families engage in active smear campaigns designed to damage your reputation and isolate you from potential sources of support. They may spread rumors about your mental health, your character, or your behavior that make others less likely to believe your perspective or offer you assistance.

These campaigns often include sharing carefully selected information about your struggles while omitting the context that explains them. They might tell others about your depression without mentioning the abuse that caused it. They might share stories about your anger without explaining the systematic mistreatment that provoked it.

The goal of the smear campaign is to ensure that if you try to tell your story, you won't be believed. By preemptively damaging your credibility, they protect themselves from accountability and maintain control over the narrative about your relationship.

The Recruitment of Others

The rejection campaign often extends beyond immediate family to include friends, extended family, and community members. The family works to turn others against you by sharing their distorted version of events and positioning themselves as long-suffering victims of your difficult behavior.

This recruitment serves to amplify their power and extend their reach. Instead of just immediate family members rejecting you, you may find yourself ostracized by entire extended family networks or community groups that were influenced by their narrative.

The isolation created by this expanded rejection is profound and intentional. It's designed to make you feel like you have nowhere to turn and no one who will believe or support you. The hope is that this isolation will force you to return to the family system and accept your scapegoat role rather than face life alone.

Surviving Emotional Abandonment

The Primal Terror of Rejection

Being ostracized by your family triggers primal fears of abandonment that go back to our earliest survival instincts. As children, family rejection literally threatened our survival. As adults, even though we can survive independently, the emotional impact of family abandonment can feel devastating and life-threatening.

This terror is normal and understandable. You're not overreacting or being dramatic. You're responding to the activation of deep survival fears that served an important purpose in human evolution. The key is recognizing these feelings as temporary responses to a real loss rather than permanent truths about your worth or future.

The grief that follows family rejection often comes in waves. You may experience denial, hoping that they'll come to their senses and welcome you back. You may feel anger at their cruelty and injustice. You may bargain, wondering if there's something you could do or say to fix the relationship. You may feel profound sadness and loss for the family you thought you had.

The Unique Grief of Family Estrangement

The grief of family estrangement is different from other types of loss because it involves the death of relationships with people who are still alive. There's no funeral, no social recognition of your loss, no clear endpoint to the grieving process.

Society tends to view family estrangement as a choice rather than a tragedy, which can leave you feeling isolated in your grief. People may suggest that you should "just forgive" or "be the bigger person" without understanding that you're grieving the loss of people who chose to abandon rather than love you.

This grief is also complicated by the simultaneous relief that many scapegoats feel when the abuse finally stops. You may feel guilty for experiencing peace alongside pain, or confused about why you miss people who treated you terribly. These conflicting emotions are normal responses to the end of complicated, traumatic relationships.

Building New Sources of Support

Surviving family abandonment requires building new sources of support and connection. This might include chosen family—friends who become like family to you. It might involve support groups for others who have experienced family estrangement. It often includes professional therapy to help process the trauma and develop healthy relationship skills.

Building new support systems takes time and patience with yourself. You may find it difficult to trust others or to believe that anyone could genuinely care about you after being rejected by the people who were supposed to love you unconditionally. This wariness is a natural protective response that served you well in your family of origin but may need to be adjusted for healthier relationships.

The process of building chosen family involves learning to recognize healthy relationship dynamics, setting appropriate boundaries, and gradually opening yourself to genuine care and support. It requires healing the internal beliefs about your worth that were damaged by your family's treatment.

The Gradual Emergence of Self

One of the unexpected gifts of family ostracization is the space it creates for you to discover who you are without the constant pressure to play your assigned role. When you're no longer performing the scapegoat function, you can begin to explore your authentic interests, values, and personality.

This emergence of self often happens gradually. You may discover interests you never knew you had because they were discouraged or dismissed by your family. You may find that you're naturally more confident, creative, or peaceful when you're not constantly managing family dysfunction or defending yourself from attack.

The freedom to be yourself can feel simultaneously exhilarating and terrifying. After years of having your identity defined by others, self-determination can feel overwhelming. It's normal to feel lost or confused about who you are when you're no longer defined by your scapegoat role.

When Going No Contact Becomes Necessary

Sometimes family ostracization makes the decision for you, but other times you may need to actively choose no contact to protect your healing and wellbeing. This decision often comes after years of trying to maintain relationships while protecting yourself from ongoing harm.

The decision to go no contact is rarely easy or sudden. It usually represents the end point of a long process of recognizing that the relationship is too toxic to maintain and that your efforts to create healthy dynamics have been consistently rejected or sabotaged.

You may reach this decision point when you realize that every interaction with family members leaves you feeling worse about yourself, when you notice that your mental health improves significantly during periods of separation, or when you recognize that their presence in your life prevents you from healing and growing.

The Guilt and Self-Doubt

Choosing no contact often triggers intense guilt and self-doubt. You may worry that you're being selfish, unforgiving, or extreme. You may question whether you're making the right choice or whether you should try harder to make the relationships work.

These feelings are normal responses to making a choice that goes against social expectations about family loyalty. The guilt is often intensified by the family's attempts to make you feel responsible for their pain or for "breaking up the family" through your absence.

It's important to remember that going no contact is not a punishment you're inflicting on others; it's protection you're providing for yourself. You have the right to remove yourself from relationships that consistently harm you, regardless of your biological connection to the people involved.

The Practical Challenges

Implementing no contact involves practical challenges beyond the emotional ones. You may need to block phone numbers, email addresses, and social media accounts. You may need to inform mutual friends and extended family about your boundaries and ask them not to share information about you.

Holidays and family events can be particularly challenging during no contact. You may need to create new traditions and find alternative sources of support during times that were previously defined by family gatherings. This requires planning and often involves grieving the loss of rituals and celebrations that had meaning for you.

Legal and financial entanglements can complicate no contact decisions. If you share business interests, property, or other legal connections with family members, you may need professional assistance to navigate these complications while maintaining your boundaries.

The Healing Space

No contact creates space for healing that's often impossible while maintaining relationships with actively harmful people. Without the constant stress of managing family dysfunction, your nervous system can begin to settle. Without regular exposure to gaslighting and invalidation, your sense of reality can stabilize.

This healing space allows you to work through trauma without new injuries being constantly inflicted. You can develop healthy relationship skills without having them undermined by unhealthy family dynamics. You can build self-esteem without it being regularly attacked by people who need you to feel worthless.

The quality of your life often improves dramatically during sustained periods of no contact. You may notice improvements in your physical health, mental clarity, creativity, and ability to form healthy relationships with others. These improvements confirm that your decision to prioritize your wellbeing was correct.

The Possibility of Future Contact

Going no contact doesn't have to be a permanent decision, though for many people it becomes one. Some individuals find that after years of healing and growth, they can maintain limited contact with some family members under carefully controlled circumstances.

Any decision about future contact should be based on evidence of genuine change in family members' behavior, not just promises or temporary improvements. It should also be based on your own emotional stability and ability to maintain boundaries rather than hope that things will be different.

The decision about whether to ever resume contact is entirely yours to make. You don't owe anyone access to your life, regardless of biological relationships. Your first responsibility is to your own wellbeing and to protecting the healing you've worked so hard to achieve.

The Freedom Beyond the Pain

Reclaiming Your Life

When love becomes hate and families choose rejection over growth, you're faced with a profound loss but also a profound opportunity. You're free to build a life based on your own values rather than their expectations. You're free to form relationships with people who appreciate your authentic self rather than people who need you to play a role.

This freedom often comes with a period of grief and adjustment, but it ultimately offers possibilities that weren't available while you were trapped in dysfunctional family dynamics. You can choose how to spend your time, energy, and emotional resources. You can pursue interests and relationships that nourish you rather than drain you.

The End of False Hope

Family ostracization, while painful, often provides clarity that ends years of false hope and wasted energy. You no longer need to wonder if this will be the year they finally see your worth. You no longer need to prepare for family events hoping this time will be different. You no longer need to manage their emotions or take responsibility for their problems.

This clarity, while painful to achieve, is ultimately liberating. It allows you to stop investing energy in relationships that were never going to provide what you needed and to redirect that energy toward healing and building genuinely supportive connections.

The end of false hope is the beginning of realistic hope—hope based on your own capacity for growth and healing rather than on other people's potential for change. This realistic hope becomes the foundation for building a life that reflects your true worth rather than their distorted perceptions.

In our final section of the book, we'll explore the healing journey that becomes possible when you're no longer expending energy on relationships that were designed to harm you. We'll look at the stages of grief specific to family estrangement, the process of reconnecting with your suppressed emotions, and the profound work of healing your inner child. Most importantly, we'll explore how to build an authentic life that honors who you really are rather than who you were forced to be.

Part IV: Healing

12

EMOTIONAL RESURRECTION

RECONNECTING WITH FEELINGS

After years of emotional suppression and survival mode, many scapegoats find themselves in a strange predicament: they know intellectually that they've been harmed, but they struggle to feel the emotions that should naturally accompany this awareness. If you've spent decades disconnecting from your feelings to survive family dysfunction, the prospect of reconnecting with them can feel both necessary and terrifying.

I remember the confusion I felt when I first began therapy. I could analyze my family dynamics with remarkable clarity, but when my therapist asked how I felt about various experiences, I often drew a blank. It wasn't that I didn't want to feel—I literally couldn't access emotions that had been shut down for so long they felt foreign to me.

This emotional numbing wasn't a character flaw or sign of weakness. It was a sophisticated survival mechanism that protected you from being overwhelmed by feelings that would have been dangerous to express in your family environment. Now that you're safe enough to begin feeling again, the process of emotional resurrection becomes a crucial part of your healing journey.

Learning to feel again safely is delicate work that requires patience, self-compassion, and often professional support. Your emotions aren't your enemies—they're sources of vital information and energy that trauma forced you to disconnect from. Reclaiming them is part of reclaiming yourself.

Connecting with Your Suppressed Emotions

Understanding Emotional Suppression

Emotional suppression in dysfunctional families isn't a conscious choice children make. It's an adaptive response to environments where expressing authentic emotions leads to punishment, ridicule, or increased danger. Your emotional suppression was a brilliant survival strategy that helped you navigate impossible circumstances.

In healthy families, children learn that their emotions are valid sources of information about their needs and experiences. They're taught to recognize, name, and express their feelings in appropriate ways. Parents help children regulate overwhelming emotions while validating their underlying experiences.

In dysfunctional families, children learn that their emotions are inconvenient, inappropriate, or dangerous. They may be punished for crying, dismissed for expressing fear, or raged at for showing anger. Over time, they learn to shut down emotional responses before they fully form, creating a protective numbness that extends into adulthood.

This suppression often becomes so automatic that adult survivors aren't consciously aware they're doing it. They may feel "fine" about traumatic memories, struggle to identify what they're feeling in the present moment, or experience emotions as physical sensations rather than recognizable feelings.

The Physical Impact of Emotional Suppression

When emotions are consistently suppressed, they don't disappear—they get stored in the body. Research on trauma and emotional suppression shows that unexpressed emotions can manifest as physical symptoms: chronic tension, digestive issues, autoimmune problems, or persistent fatigue.

Dr. Bessel van der Kolk's work on trauma demonstrates how emotional suppression affects the nervous system, creating patterns of hypervigilance, dissociation, or emotional numbing that persist long after the original threat has passed. Your body becomes a storage container for feelings that weren't safe to experience consciously.

Many survivors notice that as they begin emotional healing work, they experience temporary increases in physical symptoms. This can feel alarming, but it often represents the body beginning to release emotions that have been held for years or decades.

Understanding this connection between emotional suppression and physical symptoms helps explain why traditional talk therapy sometimes isn't enough for trauma recovery. Healing often requires body-based approaches that help release stored emotions and retrain the nervous system.

The Layers of Suppression

Emotional suppression typically happens in layers, with different emotions being shut down at different times and to different degrees. You might have maintained access to some "safer" emotions like sadness or fear while completely suppressing "dangerous" ones like anger or joy.

The emotions that were most dangerous to express in your family are often the ones most deeply suppressed. If anger led to severe punishment, you might struggle to access righteous anger even when it's appropriate and protective. If joy was met with ridicule or resentment, you might feel guilty or anxious when good things happen.

Some survivors maintain access to emotions but only in muted forms. They might feel "a little sad" about traumatic experiences that should provoke profound grief, or "somewhat annoyed" by behavior that warrants real anger. This emotional dampening served to keep feelings at manageable levels when full expression wasn't safe.

Understanding these layers helps explain why emotional reconnection is gradual work. You're not just learning to feel again—you're learning to feel at appropriate intensities and to trust that it's safe to experience the full range of human emotion.

Learning to Feel Again Safely

Creating Internal Safety

Before you can safely reconnect with suppressed emotions, you need to create internal conditions that support emotional experience. This involves developing what trauma therapists call "emotional regulation skills"—the ability to feel emotions without being overwhelmed by them.

Internal safety includes having strategies for managing emotional intensity when it arises. This might involve breathing techniques, grounding exercises, or physical movements that help you stay present with difficult feelings without dissociating or becoming overwhelmed.

It also involves developing self-compassion for whatever emotions arise. Many survivors judge themselves harshly for having "negative" emotions or worry that feeling angry, sad, or afraid means they're not healing properly. Learning to welcome all emotions as valid information is crucial for safe reconnection.

Internal safety requires patience with the process. Emotions that have been suppressed for decades won't return overnight, and when they do, they may feel intense or unfamiliar. Having realistic expectations about the timeline and nature of emotional reconnection helps prevent discouragement or self-criticism.

External Safety Considerations

Reconnecting with emotions also requires external safety—environments and relationships that support emotional expression rather than punishing it. This might mean limiting contact with people who invalidate your feelings or finding spaces where emotional expression is welcomed and supported.

Many survivors find that group therapy, support groups, or therapeutic communities provide valuable contexts for safe emotional exploration. Being around others who are also learning to feel again can normalize the process and provide encouragement during difficult moments.

It's often helpful to have professional support during intensive emotional reconnection work. Therapists trained in trauma recovery can help you navigate overwhelming emotions, provide tools for emotional regulation, and ensure that you don't become retraumatized by accessing feelings too quickly or without adequate support.

External safety also means protecting your emotional exploration from people who might use your vulnerability against you. Family members who participated in your emotional suppression may react negatively to your emotional healing, seeing it as a threat to their comfort or control.

Starting with Safer Emotions

Many therapists recommend beginning emotional reconnection work with "safer" emotions—feelings that feel less threatening or overwhelming. This might include mild sadness, gentle joy, or quiet contentment. These emotions can serve as training grounds for developing emotional tolerance and regulation skills.

As you build confidence with manageable emotions, you can gradually work toward accessing more intense or complex feelings. This progression helps ensure that you don't become overwhelmed by emotional intensity before you have adequate coping skills.

Some people find it helpful to start with emotions related to current experiences rather than diving immediately into feelings about past trauma. Learning to identify and express emotions about present-day situations builds skills that can later be applied to processing historical experiences.

The goal isn't to rush toward feeling everything at once but to gradually expand your emotional range and tolerance in a way that feels sustainable and safe.

Working with Emotional Flooding

Sometimes, as emotional suppression begins to lift, survivors experience what feels like emotional flooding—intense emotions that seem to come out of nowhere and feel unmanageable. This can be frightening, especially for people who have spent years in emotional numbness.

Emotional flooding often represents the release of feelings that have been suppressed for long periods. While overwhelming, it's usually a sign that your system is beginning to trust that it's safe to feel again. Having strategies for managing these intense emotional experiences is crucial.

Grounding techniques can help during emotional flooding: focusing on physical sensations, naming objects in your environment, or engaging in rhythmic activities like walking or breathing exercises. The goal is to stay present with the emotions rather than dissociating or becoming overwhelmed.

It's important to remember that emotions, however intense, are temporary experiences. They have a natural beginning, middle, and end if you allow them to flow without trying to stop or control them. Fighting against emotional flooding often intensifies and prolongs the experience.

Emotional Regulation and Self-Soothing

Developing Your Emotional Vocabulary

Many people who have suppressed emotions for extended periods struggle with emotional vocabulary—the ability to identify and name what they're feeling. They might know they feel "bad" or "upset" but struggle to distinguish between sadness, fear, anger, or disappointment.

Developing emotional vocabulary is like learning a new language. It takes practice and patience. Emotion wheels, feelings charts, or apps designed to help identify emotions can be valuable tools for expanding your ability to recognize and name different emotional states.

The more precisely you can identify what you're feeling, the better you can understand what that emotion is telling you and how to respond to it appropriately. Anger might signal that a boundary has been crossed. Sadness might indicate that you need comfort or support. Fear might warn you about potential danger.

Building emotional vocabulary also helps you communicate with others about your internal experiences, which is crucial for developing healthy relationships and receiving appropriate support.

Self-Soothing Techniques

As you reconnect with emotions, developing effective self-soothing techniques becomes essential. Self-soothing involves providing yourself with comfort and care during difficult emotional experiences without relying on others to manage your emotions for you.

Effective self-soothing might include physical comfort measures: warm baths, soft blankets, gentle movement, or holding comforting objects. It might involve sensory experiences: listening to calming music, smelling pleasant scents, or looking at beautiful images.

Self-soothing can also be cognitive: reminding yourself that emotions are temporary, that you're safe now, or that you have the resources to handle whatever you're feeling. Some people find comfort in mantras, affirmations, or spiritual practices.

The key to effective self-soothing is having multiple strategies available and knowing which techniques work best for different types of emotional distress. What soothes anxiety might be different from what helps with sadness or anger.

The Window of Tolerance

Trauma therapists often refer to the "window of tolerance"—the zone of emotional intensity where you can feel emotions without becoming overwhelmed or shutting down. Learning to recognize and work within your window of tolerance is crucial for safe emotional reconnection.

When you're within your window of tolerance, you can feel emotions clearly, think rationally, and make good decisions about how to respond. When you're outside this window—either in emotional overwhelm or numbness—your ability to process and integrate emotional experiences is compromised.

Part of emotional healing involves gradually expanding your window of tolerance so you can handle greater emotional intensity without becoming dysregulated. This happens through practice, support, and the development of better emotional regulation skills.

Recognizing when you're approaching the edges of your window allows you to use coping strategies before becoming overwhelmed or shutting down. This might involve taking breaks, using grounding techniques, or seeking support before emotional intensity becomes unmanageable.

Co-Regulation and Healthy Relationships

While developing self-soothing skills is important, humans are also designed for co-regulation—the process of being soothed and emotionally supported by others. Learning to both give and receive emotional support is part of healthy relationship development.

Co-regulation involves being able to remain emotionally present with others during their difficult emotions without trying to fix or change them. It also involves allowing others to provide comfort and support during your own emotional experiences.

Many survivors struggle with co-regulation because they learned that their emotions were burdens or that expressing needs led to rejection or punishment. Learning to trust others with your emotional experiences is often a gradual process that requires careful selection of supportive people.

Healthy co-regulation doesn't involve emotional caretaking or taking responsibility for others' emotional states. It involves mutual support, respect for emotional boundaries, and the ability to maintain your own emotional stability while being present with others.

Daily Healing Practices

Building Emotional Awareness Habits

Developing daily practices for emotional awareness helps make emotional reconnection a gradual, sustainable process rather than something that only happens in crisis moments or therapy sessions. Simple daily check-ins with yourself can help you rebuild connection with your emotional life.

This might involve setting aside a few minutes each day to notice what you're feeling, keeping a journal where you track emotional experiences, or using apps that prompt you to identify and rate your emotions throughout the day.

Body scan practices can help you notice emotions that might be stored physically. Taking time to slowly notice sensations in different parts of your body can help you identify emotional experiences that haven't yet reached conscious awareness.

Mindfulness practices help you stay present with emotions as they arise rather than immediately trying to change or avoid them. Learning to observe emotions with curiosity rather than judgment is a crucial skill for emotional healing.

Creative Expression

Many people find that creative expression provides a safe outlet for emotions that feel too intense or complex for words. Art, music, dance, writing, or other creative pursuits can help you explore and express emotional experiences in non-threatening ways.

Creative expression doesn't require artistic skill or talent—it's about using creativity as a tool for emotional exploration and release. The goal isn't to create something beautiful but to allow emotions to flow through creative channels.

Some people find that certain types of creative expression work better for different emotions. Drawing or painting might help with anger, while music or dancing might be better for sadness or joy. Experimenting with different creative outlets helps you discover what works best for your emotional expression.

Creative expression can also help you access emotions that are difficult to reach through talking or thinking. Sometimes emotions emerge through creative work that you weren't consciously aware you were carrying.

Movement and Embodiment

Since emotions are stored in the body, movement practices can be powerful tools for emotional reconnection and release. This doesn't necessarily mean intense exercise—gentle yoga, walking, dancing, or even stretching can help emotions move through your system.

Some people find that specific types of movement help with specific emotions. Vigorous exercise might help release anger, while gentle rocking or swaying might soothe sadness. Experimenting with different types of movement helps you discover what supports your emotional processing.

Embodiment practices help you reconnect with your body as a source of emotional information rather than just something to manage or control. Learning to listen to your body's signals and trust its wisdom is part of emotional healing.

Movement can also help when you feel stuck in particular emotions. Sometimes changing your physical position or engaging in movement can help emotions flow and transform naturally.

Building Supportive Routines

Creating daily routines that support emotional wellbeing helps establish a foundation for emotional healing. This might involve morning practices that help you start the day feeling grounded, evening routines that help you process the day's experiences, or regular self-care activities that nourish your emotional life.

Supportive routines might include meditation, journaling, time in nature, regular meals, adequate sleep, or connection with supportive people. The key is consistency—small daily practices often have more impact than occasional intensive efforts.

Building routines that support emotional wellbeing also involves identifying and modifying habits that suppress or avoid emotions. This might mean reducing alcohol use, limiting exposure to triggering media, or changing relationship patterns that prevent emotional processing.

The goal is to create a lifestyle that supports your emotional healing rather than undermining it. This often involves making gradual changes that feel sustainable rather than dramatic overhauls that are difficult to maintain.

The Return of Emotional Vitality

Rediscovering Joy and Pleasure

One of the most beautiful aspects of emotional resurrection is the return of positive emotions that may have been suppressed along with difficult ones. Many survivors discover that as they reconnect with painful emotions, they also regain access to joy, pleasure, excitement, and contentment.

This return of positive emotions can feel unfamiliar or even uncomfortable at first. You might feel guilty for experiencing joy when others are suffering, worried that happiness won't last, or afraid that expressing positive emotions will make you a target for others' resentment.

Learning to tolerate and trust positive emotions is often part of emotional healing work. You deserve to experience the full range of human emotions, including the pleasurable ones. Joy and happiness aren't luxuries reserved for people who haven't experienced trauma—they're part of your emotional birthright.

Allow yourself to notice and savor small moments of pleasure: the taste of good food, the warmth of sunlight, the sound of laughter, the comfort of a good book. Building tolerance for positive emotions often starts with these small experiences.

Emotional Integration

As your emotional range expands and you become more comfortable with feeling, you'll likely notice that you can hold multiple emotions simultaneously. You might feel both sad about what you lost and grateful for what you've gained, both angry about past treatment and hopeful about your future.

This emotional complexity is a sign of healing and integration. Life is complex, and having a full emotional range allows you to respond appropriately to the nuances of human experience. You don't have to resolve emotional contradictions or make them make logical sense.

Emotional integration also involves learning that you can feel strong emotions without being controlled by them. You can feel angry without acting destructively, sad without becoming depressed, or afraid without being paralyzed. Emotions become information and energy rather than directives you must follow.

The Gift of Empathy

As you reconnect with your own emotional experiences, you may find that your capacity for empathy—both for yourself and others—expands significantly. Understanding your own emotional

pain often creates natural compassion for others who are struggling.

This empathy becomes a gift not only to others but to yourself.
As you develop compassion for your own emotional experiences,
you're less likely to judge yourself harshly for having feelings or for
the time it takes to heal.

Your emotional resurrection also allows you to form deeper, more
authentic relationships with others. When you can feel and express your own emotions appropriately, you can also be present
with others' emotional experiences without trying to fix or change
them.

The empathy that develops through emotional healing is different
from the hypervigilance and emotional caretaking you may have
learned in your family. It's based on choice and healthy boundaries
rather than survival and obligation. You can choose when and
how to extend empathy rather than feeling compelled to manage
everyone's emotions.

In our next chapter, we'll explore the profound work of healing
your inner child—the part of you that carries the wounds from
your childhood experiences but also holds your capacity for wonder, creativity, and joy. Learning to reparent yourself with the love
and care you deserved but didn't receive is transformative work
that builds on the emotional foundation we've established here.

13

HEALING YOUR INNER CHILD

REPARENTING WORK

Within every adult survivor lives a child who never received the love, protection, and nurturing they needed to develop a secure sense of self. This inner child carries both your deepest wounds and your greatest capacity for healing, joy, and authentic connection. Learning to heal and reparent this inner child is one of the most profound and transformative aspects of recovery from family trauma.

When I first encountered the concept of inner child work, I was skeptical. It seemed too simplistic, too "new age" to address the complex trauma I had experienced. But as I began to understand that healing involves more than intellectual insight, I discovered that my inner child held keys to recovery that my adult mind couldn't access alone.

Your inner child isn't a metaphor or psychological concept—it's the part of you that holds your earliest experiences, your core wounds, and your fundamental beliefs about yourself and the world. This child part of you has been carrying pain, fear, and unmet needs for years or decades, waiting for someone to finally see and care for them properly.

Healing your inner child doesn't mean becoming childish or avoiding adult responsibilities. It means learning to provide yourself with the care, protection, and unconditional love that every child deserves but that you didn't receive. It means becoming the parent to yourself that you needed but never had.

Healing Your Inner Child: Powerful Steps

Acknowledge Your Inner Child's Existence

The first step in inner child healing is simply acknowledging that this wounded child part of you exists and has been carrying pain all these years. Many adults dismiss their childhood experiences as "over" or "in the past," not realizing that unhealed childhood wounds continue to influence their thoughts, feelings, and behaviors.

Your inner child exists in the places where you feel small, scared, or overwhelmed by life circumstances. They show up in your automatic reactions to criticism, your patterns in relationships, your fears about abandonment or rejection. They live in your dreams, your creative impulses, and your capacity for wonder and joy.

Acknowledging your inner child means recognizing that the child you once were still lives within you and still needs care and attention. This isn't weakness or immaturity—it's an acknowledgment of the complex way that human development works and the reality that childhood experiences continue to influence us throughout our lives.

Take a moment to consider: What was it like to be you as a child in your family? What did that child need that they didn't receive? What did they long for, fear, or dream about? Beginning to see this child part of yourself with compassion is the foundation for all inner child healing work.

Listen to Your Inner Child's Story

Your inner child has a story to tell—about what happened to them, how they felt, what they needed, and how they survived. This story may be different from the "official" family narrative or even from your adult understanding of your childhood. Your inner child's perspective is valid regardless of how it differs from other viewpoints.

Listening to your inner child's story often involves accessing emotions and memories that your adult mind might prefer to avoid. This child might tell you about feeling scared, lonely, confused, or invisible. They might share memories of being criticized, ignored, or forced to grow up too fast.

This listening requires patience and compassion. Your inner child might not trust you immediately—after all, they've been waiting for someone to truly hear them for a very long time. They might test you to see if you'll dismiss their feelings or blame them for their experiences the way others have.

Creating space for your inner child's story might involve journaling from their perspective, drawing or creating art that expresses their experiences, or simply sitting quietly and asking them what they want you to know. The goal isn't to fix or change their story but to witness it with love and validation.

Validate Your Inner Child's Feelings

One of the most healing things you can do for your inner child is to validate their feelings without trying to minimize, explain away, or fix them. Your inner child needs to hear that their emotions were appropriate responses to inappropriate treatment, that they weren't "too sensitive" or "making too big a deal" out of things.

Validation means acknowledging that your inner child's fear, sadness, anger, or confusion made perfect sense given what they experienced. It means affirming that they deserved better treatment and that what happened to them wasn't their fault.

This validation might sound like: "Of course you felt scared when they yelled at you. Of course you felt sad when they ignored you. Of course you felt confused when they said they loved you but treated you badly. Your feelings were completely normal reactions to abnormal treatment."

Many survivors struggle with validating their inner child's feelings because they've internalized their family's messages about being "too sensitive" or "overreacting." Learning to trust your inner child's emotional reality is part of healing the damage done by years of gaslighting and invalidation.

Apologize for Past Neglect

As you begin to understand how your inner child has been carrying pain and unmet needs, it's important to acknowledge your own role in continuing their neglect. This isn't about blaming yourself for surviving as best you could, but about taking responsibility for how you may have dismissed, criticized, or ignored your inner child's needs as an adult.

Many survivors continue the patterns they learned in childhood by being self-critical, pushing themselves beyond their limits, or dismissing their own emotional needs. Your inner child has been waiting not just for family members to acknowledge their pain but for you to stop treating them the way your family did.

This apology might sound like: "I'm sorry I didn't listen to you before. I'm sorry I pushed you so hard. I'm sorry I told you to get over things that still hurt. I'm sorry I didn't protect you or care for you the way you deserved. I want to do better now."

This step often brings up intense emotions—grief for how long your inner child has been waiting, anger at the adults who failed to protect them, or sadness for the innocence that was lost. Allow these emotions to flow without trying to fix or rush through them.

Provide Safety and Protection

Your inner child needs to know that you, as the adult, are now capable of providing the safety and protection they never had. This involves both internal safety—protecting them from self-criticism and harsh internal voices—and external safety—making choices that prioritize your wellbeing over others' approval.

Internal protection might involve interrupting self-critical thoughts and replacing them with kind, supportive messages.

When you notice yourself being harsh or demanding, you can pause and ask, "Is this how I would talk to a child I love?" Then adjust your internal dialogue accordingly.

External protection involves setting boundaries with people who are harmful or triggering, removing yourself from situations that feel unsafe, and making choices based on your own needs rather than others' expectations. Your inner child needs to see that you're willing to stand up for them in ways that the adults in your childhood couldn't or wouldn't.

This protection also involves taking care of your basic needs: eating regularly, getting enough sleep, seeking medical care when needed, and creating environments that feel safe and nurturing. Your inner child's sense of safety is built on evidence that you're capable of caring for them properly.

Meet Your Inner Child's Unmet Needs

Every child has basic emotional needs: unconditional love, acceptance, validation, safety, fun, and encouragement. Your inner child is still carrying the pain of these unmet needs and is waiting for someone to finally provide what they've been longing for.

Meeting these needs as an adult might involve giving yourself permission to play, be creative, or pursue interests that bring you joy. It might mean celebrating your achievements the way a loving parent would, or comforting yourself during difficult times the way you wished someone had comforted you as a child.

This isn't about indulging every whim or avoiding adult responsibilities. It's about bringing conscious care and attention to the legitimate needs that were ignored or dismissed during your childhood. Your inner child might need more affection, more praise, more patience, or more understanding than you received growing up.

Some people find it helpful to literally nurture their inner child by buying them something special, taking them somewhere fun, or engaging in activities that the child part of them enjoys. Others focus on meeting emotional needs through internal dialogue, affirmations, or therapeutic work.

Heal Shame and Self-Blame

Scapegoated children often internalize deep shame and self-blame, believing that they must be fundamentally flawed or bad to deserve such treatment. Your inner child may be carrying beliefs like "I'm not lovable," "I'm too much," "I'm not good enough," or "Everything is my fault."

Healing these core shame beliefs requires patience and consistent gentle correction. When these beliefs surface, you can respond with loving truth: "You are completely lovable exactly as you are. You were never too much—they were unable to handle your beautiful, big emotions. You are more than good enough. What happened was not your fault."

This healing often happens through repeated experiences of being loved and accepted for who you truly are. As you provide yourself with unconditional acceptance and surround yourself with people who value your authentic self, the shame beliefs gradually lose their power.

Shame healing also involves recognizing that your survival strategies—even the ones that seem problematic now—were brilliant adaptations to impossible circumstances. Your inner child did whatever they could to survive and maintain connection, and they deserve credit for their resilience and creativity, not criticism for their coping mechanisms.

Encourage Your Inner Child's Authentic Expression

Your inner child holds your authentic self—your natural interests, talents, preferences, and ways of being in the world. In dysfunctional families, children often learn to suppress their authentic expression to avoid punishment or to maintain whatever connection is available.

Encouraging your inner child's authentic expression involves giving yourself permission to explore interests that were discouraged, to express emotions that were forbidden, or to pursue dreams that were dismissed. This might mean taking up art, music, or creative writing. It might mean expressing anger appropriately or allowing yourself to be silly and playful.

Your inner child may need encouragement to trust that it's safe to be authentic. They may have learned that expressing their true self leads to rejection or ridicule. Start small and build trust gradually by showing your inner child that you value and support their authentic expression.

This step often involves rediscovering parts of yourself that were buried under survival strategies and family expectations. You might find interests you forgot you had, personality traits that were suppressed, or dreams that were abandoned. Welcome these discoveries with curiosity and excitement.

Create New, Healing Experiences

While you can't change what happened to your inner child in the past, you can create new experiences that provide healing and joy. This might involve taking yourself on adventures, learning new skills, forming supportive relationships, or simply spending time in environments that feel nurturing and safe.

Creating healing experiences often involves doing things that your inner child always wanted to do but couldn't. Maybe they wanted to take dance lessons, go to the beach, have a birthday party, or simply be held and comforted when they were sad. As an adult, you can provide these experiences for your inner child.

These healing experiences don't have to be elaborate or expensive. Sometimes the most healing experiences are simple: taking a nap when you're tired, eating a favorite food without guilt, spending time in nature, or allowing yourself to cry when you're sad without trying to stop the tears.

The key is conscious intention to provide your inner child with experiences of safety, joy, comfort, and love. Each positive experience helps to balance out the negative experiences they carried for so long and builds evidence that the world can be a nurturing place.

Integrate Your Inner Child Into Your Adult Life

The final step in inner child healing isn't to heal them and then forget about them—it's to integrate your inner child into your ongoing adult life. This means maintaining awareness of their needs, continuing to provide care and protection, and allowing their wisdom and joy to enrich your daily experience.

Integration means checking in with your inner child regularly: How are they feeling? What do they need? What would be fun or nurturing for them? It means including their perspective in decision-making and honoring their need for play, creativity, and emotional expression.

This integration also means protecting your inner child from people and situations that would retraumatize them. If certain people or environments trigger your inner child's pain, it's important to limit exposure or create protection strategies. Your inner child's emotional safety should be a priority in your adult decision-making.

Successful integration allows you to access both your adult capabilities and your inner child's gifts: creativity, wonder, emotional authenticity, and capacity for joy. You don't have to choose between being a responsible adult and honoring your inner child—you can be both.

Self-Compassion: Reparenting Yourself

Learning to Be the Parent You Needed

Reparenting yourself involves learning to provide yourself with the kind of care, guidance, and support that healthy parents give their children. This isn't about becoming childish or avoiding adult responsibilities—it's about developing an internal parenting voice that's kind, protective, and nurturing.

Many survivors have developed internal parenting voices that mirror their actual parents: critical, demanding, harsh, or emotionally unavailable. Reparenting involves consciously developing a different internal voice—one that speaks to you with love, patience, and understanding.

This nurturing internal parent validates your feelings, encourages your growth, celebrates your achievements, and provides comfort during difficult times. They set appropriate boundaries, make decisions based on your wellbeing, and protect you from harm. They see your full potential while accepting you exactly as you are.

Learning to be this kind of parent to yourself takes practice and patience. You may need to consciously interrupt old patterns of self-talk and deliberately choose more compassionate responses. Over time, this nurturing voice becomes more natural and automatic.

Developing Healthy Internal Boundaries

Part of reparenting involves developing healthy internal boundaries—learning to protect your inner child from your own adult stress, criticism, or unrealistic expectations. Just as good parents shield children from adult worries and responsibilities, you can learn to shield your inner child from overwhelming adult concerns.

This might mean taking breaks from stressful situations to check in with your inner child's emotional state, or consciously switching from problem-solving mode to nurturing mode when your inner child is activated. It means recognizing when you need comfort rather than solutions, play rather than productivity.

Healthy internal boundaries also involve not expecting your inner child to carry adult responsibilities or solve adult problems. Your inner child's job is to feel, play, create, and be loved—not to figure out your career, fix your relationships, or manage your finances.

Meeting Your Own Needs Without Shame

Reparenting yourself requires learning to identify and meet your own needs without shame or apology. Many survivors struggle with this because they learned that having needs was selfish, burdensome, or dangerous.

Learning to meet your own needs involves recognizing that self-care isn't selfish—it's essential. You deserve rest when you're tired, comfort when you're sad, celebration when you achieve something important, and support when you're struggling. These aren't luxuries; they're basic human requirements.

This might involve practical self-care: eating nourishing food, getting adequate sleep, taking breaks when needed, or seeking help when overwhelmed. It also involves emotional self-care: validating your feelings, speaking kindly to yourself, and surrounding yourself with supportive people.

Meeting your own needs also means learning to ask for help when you need it. Many survivors learned to be hyperindependent because asking for help led to disappointment or increased vulnerability. Learning to accept appropriate support from others is part of healthy reparenting.

Giving Yourself What You Never Received

Unconditional Love and Acceptance

Perhaps the most profound gift you can give your inner child is unconditional love and acceptance—love that isn't dependent on your performance, achievements, or behavior. This is the love that every child deserves but that many scapegoats never received.

Unconditional love means accepting yourself completely, including your flaws, mistakes, and limitations. It means loving yourself during difficult times, not just when things are going well. It means treating yourself with kindness even when you fail to meet your own expectations.

This kind of self-love often feels foreign at first, especially if you received only conditional love growing up. You may need to practice actively, consciously choosing self-acceptance over self-criticism. Over time, this unconditional self-love becomes a foundation for healing and growth.

Unconditional love doesn't mean accepting harmful behavior from yourself or others. It means loving yourself enough to make choices that serve your wellbeing and to surround yourself with people who treat you with respect and care.

Celebration and Recognition

Your inner child needs to experience celebration and recognition for who they are and what they accomplish. Many scapegoats grew up with achievements being minimized or ignored, leaving them unable to feel proud of their successes or to celebrate their progress.

Learning to celebrate yourself involves acknowledging your achievements, both big and small. This might mean treating yourself when you reach a goal, sharing good news with supportive friends, or simply taking a moment to feel proud of your progress.

Recognition also involves seeing and acknowledging your positive qualities, strengths, and growth. Your inner child needs to hear that they're valuable, talented, and worthy of recognition. This internal recognition helps build self-esteem that isn't dependent on external validation.

Celebration can be simple: taking yourself out for a special meal, buying yourself flowers, or spending time doing something you enjoy. The key is conscious acknowledgment that you and your achievements matter and deserve recognition.

Protection and Advocacy

Your inner child needs to know that you will protect and advocate for them in ways that no one did when they were actually a child. This means standing up for yourself when you're treated unfairly, setting boundaries with people who are harmful, and making choices that prioritize your wellbeing.

Protection involves both internal advocacy—interrupting self-critical thoughts and providing yourself with emotional support—and external advocacy—speaking up when you're mistreated and removing yourself from harmful situations.

This protection also extends to protecting your inner child from retraumatization. This might mean limiting contact with family members who continue to be harmful, avoiding triggering situations when possible, or seeking professional help when you're struggling.

Learning to advocate for yourself often requires overcoming conditioning that taught you to prioritize others' comfort over your own wellbeing. Your inner child needs to see that you value them enough to protect them, even when it's difficult or uncomfortable.

Inner Child Healing Exercises

Visualization and Imagery Work

Many people find visualization exercises helpful for connecting with and healing their inner child. These might involve imagining yourself meeting your child self, providing them with comfort or protection, or creating safe, nurturing environments where they can heal and play.

One common visualization involves imagining yourself going back to comfort your child self during a difficult experience. You might visualize holding them, telling them it's not their fault, or removing them from a harmful situation. These visualizations can provide profound healing and comfort.

Another approach involves creating imaginary safe spaces where your inner child can exist without fear or judgment. This might be a magical garden, a cozy room, or any environment that feels completely safe and nurturing to your inner child.

The key to effective visualization is allowing yourself to really feel the emotions that arise and to take the exercise seriously, even if it feels silly at first. Your inner child responds to genuine care and attention, not just intellectual understanding.

Letter Writing

Writing letters to your inner child can be a powerful way to communicate directly with this part of yourself. You might write letters of apology for past neglect, letters of encouragement and support, or letters that validate their experiences and feelings.

You can also encourage your inner child to write back to you, expressing their needs, fears, dreams, or feelings. This two-way communication helps build a conscious relationship between your adult self and your inner child.

Some people find it helpful to write these letters by hand, as the physical act of writing can feel more personal and intimate. Others prefer typing or even recording voice messages to their inner child.

The content matters less than the intention to communicate with love and care. Your inner child will respond to genuine attempts at connection, even if the words don't feel perfect.

Creative Expression

Creative activities can provide powerful outlets for inner child healing because they bypass the rational mind and allow for emotional expression in safe, non-threatening ways. This might involve drawing, painting, dancing, singing, or any other creative pursuit that appeals to you.

You don't need artistic skill or talent for these exercises to be healing. The goal is expression and connection, not creating something beautiful or impressive. Allow your inner child to play and create without judgment or criticism.

Some people find it helpful to create art about their childhood experiences, their inner child's feelings, or their hopes for healing. Others prefer to engage in creative activities that their inner child simply enjoys, without any specific therapeutic goal.

The key is allowing your inner child to guide the creative process rather than imposing adult expectations or judgments. Let them choose colors, subjects, or activities that feel good to them.

Physical Comfort and Nurturing

Your inner child may need physical comfort and nurturing that they never received. This might involve wrapping yourself in soft blankets, taking warm baths, getting massages, or simply holding yourself gently when you're sad.

Some people find comfort objects helpful for inner child work: stuffed animals, soft blankets, or other items that provide physical comfort and security. These aren't childish—they're tools for providing your inner child with the comfort they need.

Physical nurturing also involves taking care of your body in loving ways: eating nourishing food, getting adequate rest, moving in ways that feel good, and seeking medical care when needed. Your inner child's sense of safety is often connected to physical wellbeing.

The goal is to provide your inner child with experiences of being cared for, protected, and cherished through physical means. This helps heal the neglect and trauma stored in your body.

The work of healing your inner child is ongoing and evolving. As you grow and change, your inner child's needs may change too. The key is maintaining awareness of this precious part of yourself and continuing to provide the love, care, and protection they deserve. In our final chapter, we'll explore how inner child healing contributes to building an unbreakable, authentic life that honors all parts of who you are.

14

UNBREAKABLE

BUILDING YOUR AUTHENTIC LIFE

After walking through the darkness of recognition, understanding, and processing, you arrive at the most beautiful part of your journey: building a life that reflects your true worth rather than others' distorted perceptions of you. You're not just healing from what was done to you—you're creating something entirely new. You're becoming unbreakable not because nothing can hurt you, but because you now know your own resilience and worth.

The word "unbreakable" doesn't mean invulnerable. It means that while life may bend you, challenge you, and test you, the core of who you are remains intact. You've survived the systematic attempt to destroy your sense of self, and in doing so, you've discovered something precious: your authentic self was always there, waiting to be uncovered and honored.

Building an authentic life after family trauma isn't about creating a perfect existence or erasing the impact of your experiences. It's about creating a life that's genuinely yours—one based on your values, your interests, your needs, and your dreams rather than on the roles others assigned you or the limitations they tried to impose.

This final chapter is about transformation, hope, and the incredible possibilities that open up when you're no longer spending your energy on relationships that were designed to diminish you.

You've done the hard work of healing—now comes the joy of building.

Self-Discovery: Who Are You Really?

Beyond the Scapegoat Role

One of the most profound questions you'll face in your healing journey is: Who are you when you're not playing the scapegoat role? After years or decades of having your identity defined by others' projections and expectations, discovering your authentic self can feel both exciting and overwhelming.

Your true self was never the problem child, the difficult one, the overly sensitive person, or any other label your family attached to you. These were roles you were forced to play, not reflections of your genuine nature. Underneath all those false identities lies someone remarkable: you.

Self-discovery often begins with noticing what feels authentic versus what feels like performance. When are you most relaxed and natural? What activities make you lose track of time? What values actually matter to you, separate from what you were taught should matter? What brings you genuine joy rather than just approval from others?

This exploration takes patience because many survivors don't trust their own preferences and instincts. You may need to experiment with different activities, relationships, and ways of being to discover what truly resonates with you. Give yourself permission to try things and change your mind, to like things that others might not understand, and to be interested in whatever genuinely captures your attention.

Reclaiming Your Interests and Passions

Many scapegoats had their natural interests discouraged, dismissed, or ridiculed. You may have learned to hide what you enjoyed or to adopt interests that seemed safer or more acceptable to your family. Part of self-discovery involves reclaiming interests that were buried under survival strategies.

Think back to what captured your imagination as a child before you learned it wasn't safe or acceptable. Were you drawn to art, music, nature, books, building things, or helping others? What made your eyes light up before you learned to hide your enthusiasm?

You might discover interests you never knew you had because they were so thoroughly discouraged that you never allowed yourself to explore them. Maybe you're naturally athletic but were told you were clumsy. Maybe you're artistic but were told you weren't talented. Maybe you're naturally social but learned to hide to avoid negative attention.

Reclaiming your interests often involves overcoming internal voices that dismiss your preferences as unimportant, impractical, or selfish. Your interests matter because they're part of who you are. You don't need to justify or explain why something appeals to you—you have the right to pursue what brings you joy and fulfillment.

Understanding Your Values

Your family may have claimed to have certain values while behaving in ways that contradicted those values. They may have said they valued honesty while lying, claimed to value family while destroying family bonds, or preached kindness while practicing cruelty. This inconsistency may have left you confused about what you actually believe and value.

Discovering your authentic values involves separating what you were taught you should value from what you actually do value. This often happens through experience—noticing what behaviors in others you admire or despise, what causes you feel passionate about, what principles you're unwilling to compromise.

Your values might be similar to or completely different from your family's stated values. You might value authenticity over image, kindness over achievement, creativity over security, or justice over peace. There's no right or wrong set of values—only what's authentic for you.

Living according to your authentic values often requires courage because it may put you at odds with others' expectations. But the integrity that comes from aligning your actions with your true values is one of the foundations of an authentic life.

Developing Your Own Voice

Scapegoats often learned to silence their own voice to survive. You may have learned that expressing your thoughts, opinions, or needs led to punishment or ridicule. Developing your authentic voice—both literally and metaphorically—is crucial for building an authentic life.

Your voice includes your right to have and express opinions, to set boundaries, to ask for what you need, and to disagree with others when necessary. It includes your unique perspective on life, your humor, your way of communicating, and your contribution to conversations and relationships.

Developing your voice often starts small: expressing a preference about where to eat, sharing an opinion about a movie, or saying no to a request that doesn't feel right. As you build confidence in using your voice, you can tackle bigger challenges: advocating for yourself at work, addressing problems in relationships, or speaking up about things that matter to you.

Remember that your voice has value. Your thoughts, opinions, and perspectives matter. You have something unique to contribute to the world, and the world is diminished when you silence yourself.

From Isolation to Healthy Relationships

Learning to Recognize Healthy People

One of the most important skills you can develop is the ability to recognize healthy people—individuals who are capable of mutual, respectful relationships. After growing up in dysfunction, you may find it difficult to distinguish between people who are safe and those who might be harmful.

Healthy people have several characteristics: they respect boundaries, take responsibility for their own emotions and actions, communicate directly rather than through manipulation, and are capable of genuine empathy and care for others. They don't try to change or fix you, and they don't need you to manage their emotions or solve their problems.

Pay attention to how you feel around different people. Healthy relationships should generally leave you feeling energized, valued, and appreciated rather than drained, confused, or criticized. Trust your body's responses—if someone consistently makes you feel tense, anxious, or small, that's important information regardless of how they present themselves.

Healthy people also demonstrate emotional regulation—they can handle disappointment, conflict, or stress without becoming abusive or manipulative. They apologize when they make mistakes, respect your decisions even when they disagree, and support your growth and independence.

Building Chosen Family

For many survivors, building chosen family—people who become like family through love and commitment rather than biology—becomes an essential part of healing. Chosen family might include close friends, mentors, romantic partners, or others who provide the love, support, and connection that your biological family couldn't.

Building chosen family takes time and patience. It involves gradually opening yourself to trust and vulnerability with people who have demonstrated their trustworthiness. It means learning to give and receive love in healthy ways, to support others without sacrificing yourself, and to accept support without feeling guilty or obligated.

Chosen family relationships are based on mutual care and respect rather than obligation or duty. People choose to be in your life because they value you, and you choose to be in their lives for the same reason. These relationships can be just as meaningful and important as biological family relationships—often more so.

Remember that chosen family doesn't have to look traditional. It might be a close friend who becomes like a sibling, a mentor who becomes like a parent, or a group of friends who celebrate holidays together. What matters is the quality of care and connection, not the specific structure.

Navigating Romantic Relationships

Romantic relationships can be particularly challenging for survivors because they often trigger attachment fears and trauma responses. You may find yourself attracted to people who recreate familiar dysfunction, or you may struggle to trust people who treat you well because healthy love feels foreign.

Healing often involves learning to recognize and interrupt patterns that don't serve you. If you repeatedly find yourself in relationships with people who are emotionally unavailable, critical, or controlling, this might reflect unconscious attempts to recreate familiar dynamics in hopes of finally "winning" love from someone who can't give it.

Healthy romantic relationships are based on mutual respect, genuine care, and emotional safety. Your partner should support your healing journey, respect your boundaries, and value your authentic self. They should be capable of handling conflict constructively and of taking responsibility for their own emotions and actions.

Take your time in romantic relationships. You don't have to rush into commitment or settle for less than you deserve because you're afraid of being alone. It's better to be single and growing than to be in a relationship that undermines your healing or forces you back into survival mode.

Setting and Maintaining Boundaries

Healthy relationships require healthy boundaries—clear limits about how you will and won't allow others to treat you. For many survivors, boundary setting feels foreign, selfish, or dangerous because they learned that boundaries led to punishment or rejection.

Boundaries aren't walls that keep people out; they're guidelines that help maintain healthy relationships. They might include emotional boundaries (not taking responsibility for others' feelings), physical boundaries (controlling who can touch you and how), or time boundaries (protecting your schedule and energy).

Setting boundaries often involves saying no to requests that don't feel right, removing yourself from situations that feel unsafe, or addressing behavior that's unacceptable. It's normal for boundary setting to feel uncomfortable at first, especially if you're not used to prioritizing your own needs.

Remember that boundaries are for your protection and wellbeing, not for punishing others. People who respect you will respect your boundaries. People who consistently push against your boundaries are showing you that they don't respect your autonomy or wellbeing.

Setting Boundaries: Protecting Your Healing

Internal Boundaries

Internal boundaries involve protecting yourself from your own self-critical thoughts, perfectionist tendencies, and trauma responses. Just as you need boundaries with others, you need boundaries within yourself to maintain emotional wellbeing.

Internal boundaries might include interrupting negative self-talk, refusing to engage in self-punishment, or setting limits on how much time you spend ruminating about problems. They involve treating yourself with the same kindness and respect you would show to someone you care about.

These boundaries also involve protecting your inner child from your adult stress and responsibilities. When you're overwhelmed by adult concerns, you can create internal boundaries that shield your inner child from anxiety and allow them to feel safe and cared for.

Internal boundaries require constant practice and self-awareness. Notice when you're being harsh with yourself and consciously choose gentler responses. Set limits on negative rumination and redirect your attention to activities that support your wellbeing. Protect your energy and emotional resources just as carefully as you protect your physical safety.

CONCLUSION

YOUR JOURNEY FORWARD

As we reach the end of this book, I want you to take a moment to acknowledge something remarkable: you've taken a journey that requires immense courage. You've looked honestly at painful realities, challenged beliefs that were programmed into you from childhood, and chosen healing over the familiar comfort of denial. That takes extraordinary strength.

When you first picked up this book, you may have been questioning your own perceptions, wondering if you were "making too big a deal" of your family experiences, or hoping to find some way to fix relationships that have caused you pain for years. Now you understand that you weren't making anything up, that your experiences were real and significant, and that some relationships simply cannot be fixed because they were broken by design.

This understanding, while painful, is also profoundly liberating. You no longer need to exhaust yourself trying to earn love from people who were never capable of giving it. You no longer need to accept blame for problems you didn't create. You no longer need to minimize your own experiences to make others comfortable.

What You've Discovered

Through our journey together, you've discovered that what happened to you wasn't random bad luck or the result of your own inadequacy. It was systematic, calculated, and served specific psychological functions for the people who harmed you. Understanding this removes the burden of personal responsibility for your family's dysfunction and places it where it belongs—on the adults who chose their own comfort over a child's wellbeing.

You've learned that your emotional responses—including your anger, your sadness, and your need to protect yourself—are not only normal but healthy. Your feelings are not evidence of your weakness or oversensitivity; they're evidence of your humanity and your innate understanding that you deserved better treatment.

You've discovered that healing is possible, even from the deepest wounds. Your brain can change, your heart can heal, and your life can be rebuilt on a foundation of truth rather than the lies you were told about yourself. The person you're becoming is not damaged goods trying to be fixed but a whole person reclaiming what was always rightfully yours.

The Transformation

The transformation you've undergone through this healing process is profound. You've moved from victim to survivor to thriver. You've learned to trust your own perceptions, honor your own needs, and protect your own wellbeing. You've discovered that you are not responsible for managing other people's emotions or solving problems you didn't create.

Perhaps most importantly, you've learned that your worth is not dependent on other people's ability to see or appreciate it. Your value exists independent of external validation. You matter because you exist, not because of what you accomplish or how perfectly you perform.

This transformation doesn't mean you'll never feel pain, never struggle with relationships, or never face challenges related to your past experiences. It means you now have tools to navigate these difficulties without losing yourself in the process. You know the difference between your authentic emotions and trauma responses. You can recognize healthy people and healthy dynamics. You can protect yourself without isolating yourself.

The Ongoing Journey

Healing is not a destination but a way of traveling. The insights you've gained from this book are not endpoints but beginning points for a lifetime of continued growth and self-discovery. You'll continue to uncover layers of conditioning that no longer serve you, continue to develop your authentic voice, and continue to build relationships that honor your true self.

There will be setbacks and challenges along the way. You may find yourself temporarily falling back into old patterns during times of stress or encountering new situations that trigger unresolved trauma. This is normal and expected—healing isn't linear, and growth often happens in spirals rather than straight lines.

When these challenges arise, remember what you've learned. Return to the tools and insights that have served you. Reach out for support when you need it. Most importantly, be patient and compassionate with yourself. The same gentleness you would offer to someone else who is healing from trauma is what you deserve to offer yourself.

Your Impact on Others

Your healing journey doesn't just affect you—it ripples out to touch everyone in your life. By refusing to perpetuate cycles of dysfunction, you're changing the trajectory not just of your own life but potentially of future generations. Children who grow up with a healed parent have opportunities for healthy development that might not have existed otherwise.

Your commitment to authenticity and emotional health gives others permission to examine their own family patterns and consider making changes. Your boundaries teach others how relationships can function when they're based on respect rather than obligation. Your healing becomes a gift not just to yourself but to your community.

You may find that some people are threatened by your growth and will try to pull you back into old dynamics. This resistance doesn't mean you're doing something wrong—it often means you're doing something very right. Your healing challenges others to examine their own choices and patterns, which can be uncomfortable for people who aren't ready for that work.

Stay committed to your own wellbeing regardless of others' reactions. You cannot heal for anyone else, and you cannot sacrifice your own growth to make others comfortable with their dysfunction.

Building Your Legacy

The life you build from this point forward becomes your legacy—not just what you leave behind but what you create and contribute while you're here. This legacy might be obvious, like raising children with emotional health and security, or subtle, like being the person in your workplace who creates psychological safety for others.

Your legacy includes every relationship you build on a foundation of mutual respect, every boundary you maintain to protect your wellbeing, every moment you choose authenticity over performance. It includes the art you create, the work you do, the kindness you show, and the wisdom you share.

Most importantly, your legacy includes the example you set for anyone else who is struggling to break free from family dysfunction. Your life becomes proof that healing is possible, that families of origin don't determine destinies, and that it's never too late to choose yourself.

A Personal Message to You

I want to speak directly to you as we conclude this journey together. I see you. I see your courage in facing painful truths, your strength in choosing healing over familiarity, your determination to build a life that honors your worth. I see the child you were who deserved so much better and the adult you've become who is working to give that child what they needed.

Your story matters. Your healing matters. Your life matters in ways you may not even recognize yet. The world needs people who understand both darkness and light, who have experienced brokenness and restoration, who can offer hope to others who are finding their way out of family trauma.

You are not broken and in need of fixing. You are whole and in the process of remembering. You are not damaged goods trying to become acceptable. You are a valuable person reclaiming what was always yours. You are not the problem in your family system that needs to be solved. You are the person who had the courage to break free from a system that was designed to keep you trapped.

Your Future

As you close this book and continue forward, carry with you the knowledge that you have everything you need within you to build a beautiful, authentic life. You have the wisdom gained from your experiences, the strength developed through survival, and the compassion born from your own healing.

Trust yourself. Trust your perceptions, your feelings, your instincts, and your dreams. You have earned the right to trust yourself through the hard work of examining your past, processing your pain, and choosing growth over stagnation.

Be patient with yourself as you continue to grow and change. Celebrate small victories and be gentle with yourself during setbacks. Remember that healing is not a linear process and that every step forward, no matter how small, is significant.

Surround yourself with people who see and appreciate your authentic self. Build relationships based on mutual care and respect. Create environments that support your wellbeing and reflect your values. Live according to your own truth rather than others' expectations.

Most importantly, remember that you are unbreakable—not because nothing can hurt you, but because you've already survived the worst that family dysfunction can offer and emerged with your humanity intact. You know your own worth, you can recognize healthy people and relationships, and you have the tools to protect and nurture yourself.

Your journey from scapegoat to survivor to thriver is complete, but your life of authentic living is just beginning. The best chapters of your story are yet to be written, and you are the author.

You are worthy. You are valuable. You are enough. And your future is bright with possibility.

Welcome to the life you were always meant to live. Welcome to being unbreakably, authentically you.

WORKS CITED

Arnsten, A. F. T. (2009). Stress signalling pathways that impair prefrontal cortex structure and function. *Nature Reviews Neuroscience*, 10(6), 410–422. https://doi.org/10.1038/nrn2648

Bowen, M. (1978). *Family therapy in clinical practice*. Jason Aronson.

Cloitre, M. (2020). ICD-11 complex post-traumatic stress disorder: Simplifying diagnosis in trauma populations. *British Journal of Psychiatry*, 216(3), 129–131. https://doi.org/10.1192/bjp.2020.43

Davidson, R. J., & McEwen, B. S. (2012). Social influences on neuroplasticity: Stress and interventions to promote well-being. *Nature Neuroscience*, 15(5), 689–695. https://doi.org/10.1038/nn.3093

Donaldson-Pressman, S., & Pressman, R. M. (1994). *The narcissistic family: Diagnosis and treatment*. Jossey-Bass.

Felitti, V. J., Anda, R. F., Nordenberg, D., Williamson, D. F., Spitz, A. M., Edwards, V., Koss, M. P., & Marks, J. S. (1998). Relationship of childhood abuse and household dysfunction to many of the leading causes of death in adults: The Adverse Childhood Experiences (ACE) Study. *American Journal of Preventive Medicine*, 14(4), 245–258. https://doi.org/10.1016/S0749-3797(98)00017-8

Herman, J. L. (1992). *Trauma and recovery: The aftermath of violence — from domestic abuse to political terror*. Basic Books.

McBride, K. (2008). *Will I ever be good enough? Healing the daughters of narcissistic mothers*. Free Press.

McEwen, B. S. (2007). Physiology and neurobiology of stress and adaptation: Central role of the brain. *Physiological Reviews, 87*(3), 873–904. https://doi.org/10.1152/physrev.00041.2006

McEwen, B. S., & Gianaros, P. J. (2011). Stress- and allostasis-induced brain plasticity. *Annual Review of Medicine, 62*, 431–445. https://doi.org/10.1146/annurev-med-052209-100430

Siegel, D. J. (1999). *The developing mind: Toward a neurobiology of interpersonal experience.* Guilford Press.

van der Kolk, B. A. (2014). *The body keeps the score: Brain, mind, and body in the healing of trauma.* Viking.

Vignando, M., & Bizumic, B. (2023). Parental narcissism leads to anxiety and depression in children via scapegoating. *The Journal of Psychology, 157*(2), 121–141. https://doi.org/10.1080/00223980.2022.2148088

World Health Organization. (2019). *ICD-11: International classification of diseases (11th revision).* https://icd.who.int/

ABOUT THE AUTHOR

Lynn Nichols is a trauma-informed narcissistic abuse recovery coach, author, personal survivor, and passionate advocate for healing and empowerment. As the host of the Narcissistic Abuse Recovery Podcast and creator of the YouTube channel Wake the Elephant, Lynn has built a global community spanning over 123 countries, providing validation, resources, and hope to survivors of narcissistic abuse.

Lynn's journey began with her own experience as a family scapegoat, navigating the complex dynamics of narcissistic family systems and the profound challenges of healing from systematic emotional abuse. Her personal transformation from victim to survivor to thriver informs every aspect of her work, bringing authenticity and deep understanding to her mission of helping others break free from toxic relationships.

Published Works

Lynn is the author of several books on narcissistic abuse recovery, including:

Overcoming the Devastation of Narcissistic Abuse: How to Heal, Recover, and Take Your Life Back

Master Manipulators: Discover Covert Tactics Narcissists Devise to Manipulate, Deceive, and Control

49 Powerhouse Affirmations: Rejuvenate Your Soul and Mind After a Destructive Relationship

Her writing combines personal insight with research-backed strategies, offering survivors practical tools for recognition, healing, and building authentic lives beyond abuse.

Coaching and Healing Resources

Lynn offers 1:1 coaching for survivors of narcissistic abuse through her platform Moving Forward with Hope (movingforwardafterabuse.com). Her work extends into somatic healing through her Transformational Somatic Healing audio sessions, designed to help survivors process trauma stored in the body and move toward emotional restoration. Additional resources including an online Narcissistic Abuse Recovery course, downloadable worksheets, and an exclusive membership community are available through her platform.

Mission and Impact

Through Moving Forward with Hope, Lynn's mission is threefold:

Validate: Validate victims — now survivors and overcomers — of narcissistic abuse

Rebuild: Provide resources and encouragement toward rebuilding lives that are fulfilling and self-directed

Revolutionize: Facilitate revolutionary change to pursue dreams, visions, and intentional living

Lynn's work extends beyond personal relationships to examine how narcissistic dynamics are woven into broader cultural systems, including the intersection of narcissism with patriarchal structures, gender roles, and societal conditioning.

Podcast and Media

The Narcissistic Abuse Recovery Podcast launched in 2021 and has grown to reach listeners across every major podcast platform. Named among the Best Narcissism Podcasts of 2026 by PodRanker, the show goes far beyond surface-level recovery content.

Episodes dive deep into the complexities of narcissistic family systems, exploring roles like scapegoat and golden child, and shedding light on the pain of ostracization and family rejection. If you've been the family scapegoat—blamed, dismissed, and cast aside—this podcast validates your experience and provides a roadmap for breaking free from toxic family patterns.

The podcast tackles topics like going no contact, setting boundaries, understanding scapegoat dynamics, healing from family trauma, and uncovering covert manipulation that keeps you from thriving. Our conversations go beyond personal trauma to examine how narcissism is woven into broader cultural systems, including patriarchy's influence on gender roles and equality.

Beyond the Work

In her personal time, Lynn enjoys traveling both internationally and domestically and spending time near the beach in warm weather. She continues to expand her platform through her Substack publication and Medium articles, always seeking new ways to reach and support survivors on their healing journeys.